The Colored Cartoon

The Colored Cartoon

Black Representation in American
Animated Short Films, 1907–1954

Christopher P. Lehman

University of Massachusetts Press • Amherst

Copyright © 2007 by University of Massachusetts Press
All rights reserved
Printed in the United States of America

LC 2007020200
ISBN 978-1-55849-613-2

Designed by Jack Harrison
Set in Adobe Minion and Kabel Display
Printed and bound by The Maple-Vail Book Manufacturing Group

Library of Congress Cataloging-in-Publication Data

Lehman, Christopher P.
The Colored cartoon : Black representation in American animated short films, 1907–1954 /
    Christopher P. Lehman.
        p. cm.
Includes bibliographical references and index.
ISBN-13: 978-1-55849-613-2 (cloth : alk. paper)
1. Animated films—United States—History and criticism. 2. Blacks in motion pictures.
I. Title.
NC1766.U5L442 2007
791.43'652996073—dc22
                        2007020200

British Library Cataloguing in Publication data are available.

CONTENTS

ACKNOWLEDGMENTS

My writing of *The Colored Cartoon* has been a labor of love. I thank God for the opportunity.

I am grateful to my editor, Clark Dougan, for his encouragement and support. He has patiently and sensitively guided me through transforming early versions into a publishable book.

I thank the faculty and staff of the University of Massachusetts's Afro American Studies Department for believing in my research. John Bracey, Robert Wolff, and Ernest Allen of the University of Massachusetts and Lynda Morgan of Mount Holyoke College—offered invaluable advice and critiques. Michael Meeropol—my former colleague at Western New England College—offered moral support and allowed me to present my initial findings to his students. My current colleagues at St. Cloud State University have also given me encouragement.

I am indebted to archivists of various collections for allowing me access to important primary materials. I am truly thankful to Ned Comstock of the University of Southern California for providing access to numerous cartoon scripts. Tom Featherstone of the United Auto Workers Archives and Julie Graham of the UCLA Arts Library Special Collections also provided me with archival materials.

I conducted many interviews over the years of my research. For their time and recollections I am grateful to Robert Givens, the late Faith Hubley, the late Bill Hurtz, the late Bill Littlejohn, the late Norm McCabe, Bill Melendez, Emanuel Muravchik, the late Ray Patterson, Ray Pointer, Martha Sigall, Ken Southworth, the late Myron Waldman, the late Berny Wolf, and Jack Zander.

I thank my parents for giving me the tools to write my book. My father instilled in me a love of writing, and my mother suggested that I research and analyze the caricatured black images that I regularly saw on television. I also appreciate my brother's willingness to watch many of the cartoons with me and allow me to pitch my ideas to him.

My daughter, Imani, expresses an unceasing joy in life that inspired me to diligence in writing the book. I am extremely grateful to my wife, Yolanda, for all of her sacrifice, patience, support, and love. Because of her, *The Colored Cartoon* exists.

NOTE TO THE READER

The Internet is an invaluable resource for animation research. Images from many of the films mentioned in *The Colored Cartoon* currently appear on webpages created by scholars and aficionados of the genre. Typing the name of a cartoon character, film title, producer, or studio into any search engine will yield a list of possible sites where still images and even film clips can be found.

The website www.goldenagecartoons.com sponsors some of the pages featuring pictures of African American characters. "The Walter Lantz Cartune Encyclopedia" contains an illustrated filmography, providing stills of scenes from the "Li'l Eightball" and "Swing Symphonies" series, among others. "The Classic Felix the Cat Page" displays pictures of Pat Sullivan's pioneering silent cartoon series. "The Looney Tunes and Merrie Melodies Page" provides illustrations of the early "Bosko" films and Leon Schlesinger's cartoons with black caricatures. Jerry Beck's website www.cartoonresearch.com features images from opening sequences to Metro-Goldwyn-Mayer and Paramount cartoons, including pictures of the later "Bosko" and "Buzzy the Crow," respectively.

Some cartoons, such as the "Amos 'n' Andy" series and Schlesinger's *Coal Black an de Sebben Dwarfs* are available for viewing in full online. Others are occasionally posted at the film-sharing website www.youtube.com.

The Colored Cartoon

INTRODUCTION

The Blackness of Animation

A MERICAN ANIMATION owes its existence to African Americans. This is not to suggest that African Americans were involved in the technological development of animated film or even that they played an active role in the creation of the first cinematic cartoons. The connection between African Americans and animation was more subtle and indirect than that but nonetheless intimate and unmistakable. Early cartoons are replete with African American characters and caricatures, and such images soon became a staple of this new cultural medium. One of the first cartoons ever made in the United States, James Stuart Blackton's *Lightning Sketches* (1907), featured the metamorphosis of a racial epithet—the word "coon"—into a pair of eyes on a blackface caricature, and Metro-Goldwyn-Mayer (MGM) produced films starring a recurrent "mammy" character for over a decade. Other popular cartoon figures, such as Felix the Cat, Mickey Mouse, and Bugs Bunny, were less derogatory, but they too traced their roots to African American culture.

The question is, why? Simple racism, a deeply ingrained tradition in the United States by the turn of the twentieth century, is one obvious answer. Just as white people controlled other American businesses, they dominated the emerging motion picture industry, including animated film. But how far does that fact alone really go toward explaining the prevalence of negative African American images in early cartoons? Many early cartoonists were recently arrived European immigrants whose familiarity with black Americans and knowledge of their history was limited at best. Moreover, by their own account, at work they were just as likely to lampoon one another's ethnic backgrounds as to ridicule African Americans. Yet it was African American, not ethnic European, caricature that became commonplace on the screen.

If not the cartoonists themselves, then, was it the producers—the owners of the studios that made the films—who determined their content? If so, what were their motives and aims? The short answer to that question again seems obvious. Animated film producers wanted to make money by developing and marketing a new form of entertainment. Given that goal, it is not surprising that they looked to other popular forms of entertainment and amusement for content that would appeal to prospective customers.

By the early twentieth century, the influence of African American folktales, music, and dance was everywhere evident in American culture, from the ongoing performance of blackface minstrelsy to the enormous popularity of Joel Chandler Harris's "Uncle Remus" stories. White entertainers had blackened their faces and poked fun at African American song, dance, and speech on stage since the 1840s, and many nineteenth-century Americans considered blackface minstrelsy the nation's first original art form. Meanwhile, Harriet Beecher Stowe's 1852 novel *Uncle Tom's Cabin* caused controversy not only because of its strong abolitionist sentiment but also because minstrels easily borrowed the main characters and reduced them to caricatures: the pious slave Uncle Tom, the foolish slave Topsy, the evil master Simon Legree. Because of its adaptability, the book continued to draw readers long after the Civil War ended slavery, especially when minstrels created stage adaptations exploiting the theme of antebellum nostalgia. From the 1880s until well into the twentieth century, Harris's fictional works also enjoyed a tremendous readership. They starred a Reconstruction-era African American man teaching moral lessons to the children on his employer's plantation by using anthropomorphic animals.

Americans seemed to accept, even to like, these expressions or echoes of African American culture, but the way in which blacks were depicted usually ranged from patronizing to degrading. The painstaking attempts of minstrels to capture with accuracy the mannerisms, speech, and singing of the slaves they had observed later evolved into vulgar caricaturing of African Americans and their enslavement. This "love and theft" of the culture had political overtones, according to the historian Eric Lott. Minstrels were initially working-class performers who appropriated certain characteristics of oppressed blacks in order to express their own discontent. The performances changed, however, as the nation increasingly debated slavery and a growing number of free blacks moved north, where they competed with disgruntled whites for jobs. Professional troupes played into their audiences' racial stereotypes of African Americans by portraying them as childlike, unintelligent buffoons who enjoyed their status as chattel. Long after minstrelsy died, the political manipulation of the black image lived on.[1]

Some aspects of the history of animation appear to support Lott's thesis. For instance, Max Fleischer, the producer of the "Betty Boop" cartoons, loved African American jazz and featured it in many of his films. Walt Disney is a somewhat more problematic case, but he also drew on African American images and motifs in ways that were not overtly racist. Although the cartoon character Mickey Mouse had his origins in blackface, Disney gradually transformed him into a racially neutral cultural icon. Warner Brothers Cartoons director Fred "Tex" Avery offers perhaps the best example of "love and theft" at work, deriving from African American folktales characters (including the immortal Bugs Bunny) who rebelled against convention and mimicked the "cool" posture of black bebop performers—a style imitated in other forms of pop culture during the 1930s and 1940s.

At the same time, however, the early history of animation contains countless examples of outrageously racist cartoon images that belittled, desexualized, infantilized, and ultimately dehumanized African Americans—images that reflected more ignorance and contempt than "love" of any sort. Slave characters tap-danced on auction blocks or skipped on their way to the slave market in chains. Lazy African American cotton-pickers sought assistance just to exhale smoke or scratch their heads. "Mammy" characters in distress needed the help of their employers' pet animals to save them. In short, the function and significance of racial imagery in the early history of American animated films is even more complicated and ambiguous than in other forms of popular culture. Unlike other film genres, animation relies on caricature—on the distortion of physical attributes and the fanciful representation of reality. Moreover, for many years all animated films were comedic. The medium had its origins as an act in vaudeville shows, and as it developed, audiences came to expect cartoons to be funny—and funny, in an art form based on caricature, usually means ridicule. Since the vast majority of movie patrons during the first half of the twentieth century were white, it may simply have been easier, or at least less risky, for producers to make African Americans the targets of ridicule and derision than any group of whites. Besides, since African Americans played no role in the animation industry—financial, artistic, or otherwise—they were not in a position to challenge or change the choices that producers and animators made.

Still, things did change. The representation of African Americans in animated film gradually evolved over time, becoming less blatantly racist and derogatory by the 1950s. Was this because an appreciation for black culture had grown among white Americans during this period? Or was it because the social, economic, and political status of black Americans gradually improved? Were African Americans gaining agency and becoming a stronger, more influential force in national life?

The purpose of this book is to explore these questions—to shed fresh light on the place of race in modern America life by examining its role in a cultural medium that first came into being at the dawn of the twentieth century. Drawing on a wide range of sources, including interviews with former animators, archived cartoon scripts, and the films themselves, I begin by looking at the white interpretations of African Americans in popular culture that the first cartoon studios set to animation. I then examine the effect of sound synchronization on animated representation of African Americans. Next I discuss the powerful control of Hollywood distributors over the content of cartoons in the late 1930s and show how these companies influenced images of African Americans. My focus then turns to the uniqueness of Bugs Bunny as a character with distinct roots in African American culture despite the lack of ethnic stereotyping in his characterization. After that, I explore the studios' updating of generalizations about African Americans through language and costume during World War II. I assess the efforts of liberal activist groups to censor the cartoons containing these images. Finally, I show how the cartoon industry finally abandoned African American caricatures during the 1950s after having exploited the ethnic group ever since the era of silent films at the turn of the century.

ONE

The Silent Era

During the first two decades of American animation (1907–27), the medium evolved from a vaudeville act to a film genre noticed by respected critics and exploited by a few Hollywood-based distribution companies. These cartoons were produced mostly in New York City, at first by individual animators but later by teams of illustrators working in studios. In terms of technical quality, they were black-and-white silent films usually running seven minutes long. Some cartoons offered character dialogue as on-screen words or "titles" enclosed in "speech balloons," like those in newspaper comic strips, but because of the absence of sound, animators generally relied on physical humor and pantomime to carry their films.

These pioneers in animation made two different types of cartoons in the years before 1920. Some studios attempted to animate comic strips that audiences had already embraced in newspapers. They hoped to cash in on the previously established popularity of the characters by making them "move" for audiences. Other companies combined live action with animation, creating the effect of an animator interacting with his cartoon characters. In both cases the animators promoted the "motion" of the drawn figures as a novelty act. The films were usually seen on vaudeville stages, and the animators often served as their own distributors, contracting with theater owners to arrange for the exhibition of the cartoons.

The New York-based newspaper cartoonist and vaudeville performer J. Stuart Blackton, one of the first animators, used several creative and financially practical production tricks that later became staples of animation. His first film, *Humorous Phases of a Funny Face* (1906), featured Blackton drawing faces on a blackboard; the faces then appeared to contort into various images. This illusion of the drawing changing itself was a result of the "trickfilm" method, in which the filmmaker filmed an image, stopped filming, changed the image, and then resumed filming. It was not only an innovative technique but an economical one as well, since filming people was much less expensive than animating drawings. By showing his hands creating the drawings, he visually presented himself to viewers as the magician giving life and movement to the sketches. Successive cartoons over the next twenty years, especially Max Fleischer's "Out of the Inkwell" series in the 1920s, borrowed Blackton's techniques of sketch "trickfilm," the combination of live action with animation, and image metamorphosis.[1]

The newspaper cartoonist Winsor McCay, whose comic strip "Little Nemo" had a large following in the 1900s, appropriated Blackton's concept of the animator as life-giver for his cartoons, but in a radically different manner from that of his predecessor. He sketched on paper instead of a board. For *Gertie the Dinosaur* (1914) he did not film himself with his star. Instead, he appeared on a vaudeville stage for an exhibition of the film, cracking his whip at the screen in synchrony with moving sketches in which the title character appeared to respond to his commands. His act won rave reviews, leading to a spate of theatrical bookings. Whereas Blackton was the star of his films and drew multiple figures, McCay made Gertie the sole star of his film. The dinosaur, as a result, became American animation's first popular character.[2]

McCay also differed from Blackton in the way he created the illusion of movement in his drawings, adding background scenery along with the characters. Although the backgrounds were relatively minimal, McCay had to copy each scene precisely from drawing to drawing in order to simulate motion on film. It was painstaking, time-consuming work, requiring thousands of drawings for each cartoon. But the inclusion of scenery that moved advanced the medium as an art form.[3]

Other innovations soon followed. In the same year that *Gertie the Dinosaur* wowed viewers and inspired other animators, the illustrators John Bray and Earl Hurd forever changed animated film by inventing the process of celluloid animation. By drawing characters on transparent celluloid sheets, or "cels," animators no longer had to redraw entire backgrounds. They did not even have to redraw the entire character itself but could merely draw those parts that the animators wanted to "move" in different positions. Animation suddenly became much less expensive to produce, and Bray and Hurd became wealthy by forming a company together and patenting their invention, thus requiring animators to pay a licensing fee to use cels.[4]

In addition to finding the key to cost-cutting in animation, Bray also raised standards in relation to distribution. In 1913 he secured a contract with Charles Pathé, whose Pathé Film Exchange was the world's largest movie production and distribution company. Pathé agreed to release Bray's "Colonel Heezaliar" series—episodes starring a fictional spinner of exaggerated yarns—to theaters nationwide. Pathé's enthusiasm for the animation medium was exceptional, for cartoons attracted few major distributors in the 1910s. Most animators had to settle for contracts with states-rights distributors, who sold prints to brokers who in turn distributed the cartoons to theaters in a specific region of the United States. Bray now demonstrated, however, that better arrangements were possible.[5]

If many of the techniques used in early animation were relatively unsophisticated, much of the content was also crude. Ethnic jokes, including many that were overtly racist or anti-Semitic, were commonplace. For example, Blackton's second film, *Lightning Sketches* (1907), featured a pair of visual ethnic puns. The animator appeared on screen to write the African American slur "coon" and the surname "Cohen" on a board. Then the word "coon" transformed into a blackface minstrel caricature, while "Cohen" took the shape of a face with a large nose. The gag itself was not central to the cartoon since the film had no plot. The scene was merely one of several metamorphosis jokes, as in *Humorous Phases of a Funny Face*. For the cartoonist to weave ethnic generalizations into his film, however, implied that somehow they belonged there.

Blackton's use of black and Jewish stereotypes reflected both his own roots in vaudeville and the prevailing cultural climate of his time. The African American caricature in his "coon" gag, formally attired in jacket and bowtie, was clearly intended to evoke the blackface minstrels of the vaudeville stage. This image also exemplified the intolerance of an increasing number of white Protestants toward recent European and Asian immigrants, Catholics, Jews, and African Americans. This hostility, or nativism, intensified during World War I against German Americans; many Americans shunned them and accused them of subversively working for the German government. The nativists considered an immigrant's assimilation into American society and removal of ethnic signifiers such as language and dress essential to establishing proof of loyalty to the United States. By the 1920s nativism had grown more violent with the emergence of xenophobic vigilante groups such as the Ku Klux Klan, which had recently redefined itself as anti-foreigner after having targeted mostly African Americans and Republicans during the previous century. Blackton shared in this nativism, either because he was not himself an immigrant or because he identified with the ruling white Protestant majority.[6]

Ethnic stereotypes persisted as a staple of cartoon humor even after immigrants themselves began to work as illustrators and animators. In 1916 two popular newspaper comic strips that were heavily reliant on ethnic humor became animated series: "The Katzenjammer Kids," starring the children of a fictitious European American immigrant family, and cartoonist Harry Hershfield's "Abie the Agent," the first Jewish cartoon star. Several East Coast illustrators, inspired by the commercial success of Blackton and McCay, became cartoon producers, hiring other people to animate the cartoons they funded. The newspaper cartoonists and illustrators employed by the New York studios in the 1910s were mostly first- and second-generation European Americans. Perhaps they were using the new medium as a form of catharsis in their struggle to assimilate into American society, allowing them to vent their frustrations through poking fun at their co-workers' ethnic identities by constructing characters based on one another's ethnic stereotypes. Or maybe the ethnic humor provided a way of distancing themselves from their own immigrant origins and identifying with the dominant culture. Whatever their motives, there was still one major difference between their films and Blackton's. Through ethnic caricature the immigrant animators acknowledged their own status as American "others." *Lightning Sketches*, by contrast, was not autobiographical; Blackton was neither a "coon" nor a "Cohen."

Within the studios, a spirit of tolerance toward ethnic caricatures seems to have prevailed among co-workers. If animators objected to their representations, either they did not outwardly say so, or else their protests fell on deaf ears. The animator Shamus Culhane, for example, claimed that the hook-nosed Jewish character he drew for a cartoon had the approval of his Jewish colleagues. The cartoonists often stated that their drawings did not result from malice toward other ethnic groups but rather grew out of a playful context; after all, they shared the bond of immigrant status, with all the anxieties and uncertainties that entailed. As the animator Jack Zander recalled, "We got a great kick out of making the worst drawings we could of each other." Yet he also acknowledged the potential for hurt feelings among the artists: "Heaven knows we drew characters of each other that were devastating. Insults, if one was to be sensitive."[7]

The caricatures the animators drew of one another did not, however, include African Americans, for the simple reason that throughout the first half of the twentieth century, no animation studio employed a black illustrator. As a result, images of African Americans tended to be especially derogatory, showing little of the playfulness associated with other ethnic cartoons. Zander explained: "Way back in the twenties, black people were repeatedly drawn in cartoons. We blatantly drew the characters with thick lips and even went as far as putting bones in the hair and noses. Gross, I will admit, but then . . . the attitude of the viewer seemed to be more tolerant." Also, the African American characters came from American popular culture instead of relationships among animators. The culture, in turn, came from media outlets dominated not by African Americans but by white people—books, plays, and movies. Consequently, although artists' European American designs varied from studio to studio, the images of the sambo, mammy, and other hoary African American caricatures from American literature, stage, and film were fairly consistent.[8]

More often than not, cartoon representations of blacks derived from traditions and stereotypes familiar to popular audiences. Pat Sullivan's "Sammy Johnsin" series, which first appeared in 1916, offers a case in point. Based on the "Sambo and His Funny Noises" newspaper strip he had illustrated for its writer, William Marriner, earlier in the decade, the series featured an African American boy living on a plantation with his mammy-like mother. Sullivan changed his protagonist's name to avoid copyright infringement, since his former boss owned the strip. But the origins of the character's name actually went back further than that, to Helen Bannerman's enormously popular *Story of Little Black Sambo*, the tale of an African boy chased by Indian tigers in a tropical rainforest. Bannerman's sale of her copyright in 1899 helped make possible not only the creation of Sullivan's comic strip but also, eventually, the publication of nearly thirty English-language versions of the book by different authors and illustrators. Sambo proved a geographically adaptable character, sometimes depicted as an African boy and at other times as an African American boy living in the rural South.[9]

The title character of "Sambo and His Funny Noises" was the latest image of the dimwitted, gullible, helpless African American boy, a stock character in much of nineteenth-century American literature. Traditionally the image served to reinforce assumptions of white superiority and undermined the efforts of African Americans seeking emancipation before the Civil War and the right to vote after the war ended. For his comic strip, Marriner transformed Sambo into a gullible Southern dupe who falls for the pranks of white neighborhood boys. The content of each adventure usually consisted of the pranksters' hiding behind a fence or tree while waiting for Sambo to approach their trap. Sambo then proceeds to fall victim to the gag, the jokesters laugh at his expense, and in the end Sambo retreats.

Sullivan made "Sammy Johnsin" quite dissimilar from "Sambo and His Funny Noises." The focus shifted from nativist humor to juvenile fantasy. In the "Sammy" films, the young boy fantasizes of traveling to distant lands such as Mexico or performing heroic deeds like hunting animals and fighting cannibals. The image of Sammy as a dreamer revealed an African American character capable of thought and reflection. He does not merely react with dim comprehension to the situations in which he finds himself; instead, he imagines an alternative reality, one in which he is a hero and an adventurer. To be sure, none of Sammy's fantasies ever reaches fruition. Inevitably, he awakes at the end of each episode, realizes that he has been dreaming, and resumes life as a poor African American boy in the rural South with no hope whatsoever of becoming a great hunter of international game, as in his dream in *Sammy Johnsin—Hunter* (1916), or of catching the imagined outlaws of *Sammy Johnsin in Mexico* (1916). Nevertheless, the contrast between Sammy's active imagination and his oppressive social circumstances is a central feature of Sullivan's films, lending his protagonist an implicit agency not found in many early-twentieth-century representations of blacks. Even before working on the "Sammy Johnsin" series, Sullivan had presented this unique variation on the juvenile African American boy. According to comic-strip historian Fredrik Stromberg, Sullivan occasionally worked simultaneously as both illustrator and substitute writer for "Sambo and His Funny Noises," and Sambo's intellect and independence significantly increased in Sullivan's editions of the strip.[10]

If Pat Sullivan was less racist than many other illustrators of his day, his

"Sammy" films were still a product of the era of nationwide segregation, Southern lynchings, and urban race riots. The proper "place" of African Americans in these cartoons remained the rural South. Sammy, living on a plantation with only his mammy-figure mother, was no exception. Also, for all his bold imaginings, Sammy never comes across as someone deserving of equality with whites or full citizenship. The conclusion of each film is quite literally, to quote the African American poet Langston Hughes, a "dream deferred."

The stories and styles of humor devised by pioneers like Sullivan for cartoons did not drastically change through the 1920s. Animators still appeared on screen with their cavorting creations and found new comic strips to "bring to life" on film. Although Blackton, McCay, and other pioneers of the medium had ceased making cartoons by that time, a new generation of animators, familiar with the films of their predecessors, kept the medium alive. Animated ethnic humor also survived the 1920s as studios continued to attract first- and second-generation American illustrators. Their cathartic ethnic stereotypes remained integral to animation. When the Austrian American Fleischer brothers opened a studio thirty years after their family had escaped persecution of Jews in their homeland, the films created by Max (the producer), Dave (the director), and Charles (the technician) Fleischer often featured caricatures of Jewish Americans and African Americans.

The Fleischer Studio was part of an expansion of the industry in New York during the 1920s. Several cartoon studios opened there, and many of the new producers came directly out of Bray's studio. Paul Terry—Bray's head animator from 1915 to 1916—later made a name for himself as the creator of the long-running "Aesop's Fables" series and as the producer of his own studio from 1930 to 1955. Terry's successor at the Bray Studio, Max Fleischer, had already departed in 1921 to open his own animation company with his brothers. In addition to animators drawing the movements of figures, studios now employed people to perform numerous other tasks such as inking the animators' sketches onto cels and making sure that the scenery did not bleed through the inked figures. Studios still hired newspaper cartoonists and illustrators for these jobs; no animation schools existed at that time.[11]

Two other members of the 1920s generation of animation—producer

Pat Sullivan and animator Otto Messmer—originated a style of cartooning that broke new ground in the medium. They popularized anthropomorphism and introduced surrealism to the American cartoon. With their "Felix" series (1919–29)—featuring a cat who expresses complex human emotions and behaviors and can walk on two legs—Sullivan and Messmer developed American animation's first popular anthropomorphic animal star. To be sure, animators had tried but failed to produce successful humanized animal stars in the 1910s. The first animal cartoon series—Robert Sidney Smith's "Old Doc Yak," John Bray's "Police Dog," Johnny Gruelle's "Quacky Doodles Family," and even an animated adaptation of George Herriman's phenomenally popular "Krazy Kat" strip—each lasted no more than three years. Felix differed from his predecessors in that Sullivan and Messmer did not settle merely for making the sketches of the feline move; they allowed him to skate "on the furthest edge of plausibility," according to the film critic Creighton Peet, who explained in 1929, "When necessary, Felix's tail becomes detachable and can be used for a walking stick, a harpoon for whales, or, by means of a little stretching, as a rope for lassoing bulls, elephants or mountains, and when the job is done, the tail modestly fastens itself back in the proper place."[12]

Felix's face as conceived by Sullivan and Messmer—resembling the blackface of minstrels—established a link between character design and African American caricature. Animators commonly used animal and African American figures with jet-black bodies and large white eyes and lips, thus avoiding the need to draw intricate details for each character on every sheet of paper or celluloid. In addition, the whiteness of the eyes and lips provided contrast with the bodies and made those facial features easier for animators to delineate. Still, the resemblance to the makeup of blackface minstrels did not go unnoticed; animators often had their animal stars break out of character and perform African American stereotypes for laughs.

Paul Terry—who worked as an illustrator in San Francisco and then in New York before a viewing of *Gertie the Dinosaur* inspired him to enter the field of animation—was a major beneficiary of blackface character design. Shortly after the "Felix" cartoons first appeared in theaters, he began animating "Aesop's Fables" episodes for the producer Amadee Van Beuren, distributed by Pathé (1919–28). The films did not have a popular recurring character, but in every episode humanized animals performed parodies of fairy tales. His characters had inky bodies and oversized eyes and lips reminiscent of Felix. The simplicity of the designs, however, enabled Terry to churn out one "Aesop's Fables" episode per week—more than five times the number of films made by Sullivan and Messmer. African American caricature thus contributed to the first of several cost-cutting animation techniques, allowing Terry to maximize profits throughout his three decades as a cartoon producer-director.

Terry's motivation for combining African American caricature with anthropomorphism was not only to capitalize on the efficiency of blackface design. He also wished to avoid reproducing the nativist content his predecessors had used in animation, though even this decision involved monetary concerns. According to the film historian Leonard Maltin, Terry chose to work exclusively with blackface animal characters because animals lack ethnicity. If no one could complain that an episode contained ethnic stereotypes, it stood little chance of offending people. More important, the absence of offensive content meant that there would be no campaigns to have Terry's films withdrawn from theaters, resulting in a loss of income from rental fees. This keen business logic helped make Terry wealthy as a cartoon producer after he left Van Beuren to start his own Terrytoons Studio in the late 1920s. Still, the fact that he was worried about offending specific groups suggests that animation studios had already come to rely too much on ethnic humor in the first decade of the medium's existence.[13]

In the 1920s blackface design was a cash cow for studios. Problems facing animation companies regarding the unauthorized duplication of their animal characters provided one of the earliest demonstrations of the tremendous financial value of African American representation to the cartoon industry. Between 1920 and 1925, Sullivan and "Felix the Cat" distributor Margaret Winkler vigorously protected their phenomenally popular black-furred, white-mouthed star from imitators. Terry was the boldest of them, featuring his own ink-colored cat named Felix in episodes of "Aesop's Fables" before he changed the animal's name to Henry and fattened its stomach. Later, the Kansas-based cartoon producer Walt Disney had to make alterations to his creation Julius the Cat after a meeting with Sullivan. In the 1930s Disney took protection against copyright infringement one step further when, this time as a plaintiff, he sued the Aesop's Fables Studio for designing cartoon mice strongly favoring his own Mickey and Minnie.[14]

By the time Mickey Mouse debuted in theaters in November 1928—the second sound-synchronized cartoon ever made—animators had already begun to draw more from traditional African American representation than from images of any other ethnic group in American media. In addition to blackface designs for metamorphosis gags and for animal characters, studios also used popular songs to accompany cartoon gags that drew laughs at the expense of African Americans. The melodies had entertained audiences since the mid-nineteenth century, and they cost nothing to use because they were in the public domain. American popular music associated with European American ethnic groups was relatively rare and far less familiar than the well-established blackface minstrel songs.

Although cartoons still lacked sound, music directors at cartoon studios provided sheet music for piano accompanists at theaters. Animators, meanwhile, synchronized their animation to the notes and lyrics. Throughout the 1920s the Fleischer Studio animated several cartoons set to blackface minstrel songs, four of which—*Dixie* (1925), *My Old Kentucky Home* (1926), *Old Black Joe* (1926), and *Oh Suzanna*—were released within months of one another over a two-year period.[15]

Fleischer's minstrel tune animations served as a bridge connecting the genre's past to its future. The films borrowed Blackton's metamorphosis technique by turning the songs' written lyrics into figures illustrating the words. These silent musicals also foreshadowed the significant role of African American representation in sound-synchronized animation. The Fleischers' innovation unwittingly paved the way for Disney's blackface musicals starring Mickey Mouse, which would dazzle critics and audiences and give the New York studios formidable competition in the sound-synchronization era.

TWO

The Arrival of Sound

Between 1928 and 1934, the animation industry redefined itself with the introduction of sound synchronization. Although America's movie industry quickly embraced sound after the phenomenal success of the first "talkie," *The Jazz Singer*, in 1927, animation studios greeted the new technology with mixed feelings. Producers Walt Disney and Max Fleischer were the most willing to animate to sound; they released their first sound cartoons within the next two years. Pat Sullivan was reluctant to do so and discontinued production of "Felix the Cat" in 1929; the following year he grudgingly added soundtracks to earlier, silent "Felix" cartoons, whose designs lacked the sophistication and polish of new cartoons from his competitors. An equally stubborn Paul Terry refused to animate "Aesop's Fables" to sound and was unceremoniously fired from his job at Amadee Van Beuren's studio in 1929 after a decade of service.

Another early casualty of the sound era was the live-cartoon film starring the animator with his character. In silent films, cartoonists could justifiably claim to have created their characters; no matter how the figures moved, the artists always had complete control over them by the power of their pens. Sound, however, added a new dimension to animation beyond the concept of pen-and-ink drawings coming to life. Animators could not take responsibility for the way the characters talked or the music playing during the scenes. Except in rare cameos, studios chose not to have the animator, the music director, and a voice actor all appear in live action, interacting with the cartoon character.

The introduction of dialogue posed problems for animators. Since most preferred to animate characters to music, the majority of cartoons produced in this period were musicals. Creating the illusion of a talking mouth was not easy. Illustrators found they had to freeze a character's actions in order to focus deliberately on the figure's lip formations as it spoke, creating the impression that characters could not move and talk at the same time. Scenes of characters singing and dancing fared better, because movements could be more easily synchronized to the rhythms of the music.

The dominance of the musical in early sound animation also arose from commercial concerns. Hollywood distributors contracting with cartoon producers often insisted that the films feature tunes owned by the distributors. When Warner Brothers Pictures commissioned "Looney Tunes" in 1930 and "Merrie Melodies" in 1931 from co-producers Hugh Harman and Rudolf Ising, each cartoon featured a dance routine based on a Warner-owned song. The Harman-Ising Studio timed the films on written music sheets and often did not begin animation until after the music director had prerecorded the score. The very names of the series emphasized the musical nature of the films. Advertisements for "Looney Tunes" similarly focused on promoting music rather than animated comedy. With particular redundancy, one flyer called the films "a brand new series of Vitaphone Song Cartoons based on current musical hits," "merry adventures . . . to the rhythm of the biggest song hits," and "a wow of an exploitation tie-up with Radio, Phonograph and Songs."[1]

African American culture once again played a central role in the evolution of the medium. From the outset of sound synchronization, animators relied heavily on the minstrelsy tradition for their music. Disney was among the first to do so. Although he was initially inspired by the success of *The Jazz Singer* to animate to sound, his reliance on minstrelsy content for his groundbreaking films mirrored Blackton's use of blackface to inaugurate animation itself. When Disney's cartoons won rave reviews, competing producers made derivative films that exploited blackface in a similar manner.

The influence of blackface minstrelsy is especially evident in the earliest cartoons starring Disney's most popular character, the jet-black, white-mouthed Mickey Mouse. Years before Mickey's falsetto voice became such a recognizable aspect of his characterization, Disney used songs commemorating African American bondage so frequently that they became the "Mickey Mouse" sound. In 1928 he constructed his first sound film—the "Mickey Mouse" cartoon *Steamboat Willie*—around "Turkey in the Straw," which was, in turn, an instrumental version of "Zip Coon"—a popular song since 1834 and the closing number for many minstrel shows. Through the scores arranged by Disney's music director Carl Stalling, Mickey also performed to the melodies of "Old Folks at Home" (in *Mickey's Follies*, 1929) and Dan Emmett's "Dixie" (in *Mickey's Choo-Choo*, 1929). These cartoons were set in rural locales such as farmyards and plains, reflecting the Kansas environment from which Disney and many of his staff originated before moving to California. Associated as they were with a romanticized vision of the antebellum South, these songs provided a perfect musical complement to the animated images of barns and riverboats. Even for episodes set outside the antebellum South, Disney used the music to define Mickey's roles. *Galloping Gaucho* (1929), set in South America, incongruously features the Civil War tune "Jubilo." A favorite among Union soldiers, this song about a slaveholder fleeing as federal troops approach plays as Gaucho Mickey arrives at a saloon to liberate Minnie from an unwelcome suitor.

Within two years, Disney's contemporaries in the industry had created their own blackface-derived anthropomorphic animals and were scoring their films with minstrel tunes. In what seemed a major coup at the time, in 1930 Metro-Goldwyn-Mayer arranged to distribute films produced by Ub Iwerks, Disney's former right-hand man and the animator for *Steamboat Willie*. His "Flip the Frog" character, however, lacked sufficient distinction from Mickey. One episode—*The Cuckoo Murder Case* (1931)—even followed the lead of *Galloping Gaucho* by using the tune "Jubilo" in a setting outside the pre–Civil War South.

Disney and other producers laid the foundations for the sound cartoon by integrating the acts of contemporary minstrels into their films. Al Jolson was the minstrel of choice; he had brought African American caricature to sound film through his starring role in *The Jazz Singer* as Jack Robin, a Jewish immigrant who uses blackface performance as a means of American assimilation. Jack's predicament was similar to that of the immigrant animators who used blackface and other forms of ethnic humor in creating a new American art form. The most enduring image of Jolson in the movie—kneeling on a stage while singing "My Mammy," his face darkened by burnt cork—appeared in numerous cartoons from Disney and the Harman-Ising Studio, which shared *The Jazz Singer*'s distributor, Warner Brothers.

The animated references to Jolson spoke to the enduring popularity of blackface minstrelsy and the first sound films. In this respect the cartoon medium served as a cultural bridge connecting the nineteenth century to the twentieth. Jolson's "mammy kneel" was so familiar to audiences that studios referred to it in settings far from the vaudeville stage of *The Jazz Singer*. A big-lipped black spider in an ancient pyramid mimics Jolson in this way in Disney's *Egyptian Melodies* (1931). Harman-Ising's cartoon *The Shanty Where Santa Claus Lives* (1933), set in a toy store, features a white baby doll that says "Mama" before falling into a bucket of soot. She emerges from it in blackface and utters "Mammy."

Harman-Ising's blackface-derived human character Bosko (also written as "Bosco") was, like his live-action counterpart Jolson, a blackface performer selling Warner Brothers films to theater audiences. The former Harman-Ising animator Jack Zander confirmed, "Bosco was obviously a little black boy, had a black face and thick lips, and his girlfriend was black also." Bosko's "Looney Tunes" episodes, however, lacked stereotypical settings such as plantations, and he did not play servile roles. Also, the songs promoted in his films were derived not from minstrelsy or any African American genre such as jazz or blues but from corporate show tunes lacking ethnic signifiers. Warner Brothers deemphasized the ethnic connotations of Bosko's blackface design in order to adapt the character to the stories constructed by Harman-Ising for each song. Neither the studio nor the distributor promoted him as an African American caricature. Though insisting that Harman and Ising "didn't do 'black' things," Zander remarked, "No one admitted openly that [Bosko] was a little black boy but it was true."[2]

Critics accustomed to minstrelsy-derived gags for blackface cartoon characters did not know what to make of Bosko's lack of ethnic signifiers. He had the same facial design as those of animal stars Mickey Mouse and Felix the Cat, and he behaved like them. As a result, reviewers disagreed as to whether Bosko was a black caricature or an animal figure. Writing about a song the character performs with a pig in *Box Car Blues*, a reviewer for *Variety* called the performance an "animal duet." Another critic for *Variety*, reviewing *Congo Jazz*, referred to Bosko as a "mutt.". Studio animators offered little help to confused viewers, as Zander recalled: "There was, in fact, a joke about who or what Bosko was. We had a cleaning man or 'handy man' or whatever who used to hang around the studio and he asked me one day, 'You got Mickey the Mouse and Felix the Cat but Bosko the What?' I couldn't answer."[3]

Bosko was too nondescript to pose a challenge to conventional African American representation. Contrary to the usual clownish roles for black cartoon characters, he was cast as a heroic figure in several episodes. He plays a pilot in *Dumb Patrol* (1930) and a World War I soldier in *Bosko the Doughboy* (1931). His roots in blackface minstrelsy are apparent only in his design. He does not speak in "Negro dialect" while flying his plane, nor does he sing a minstrel song while fighting in World War I. Thus, no reviewer identified him as a black character breaking from standard racial images. The very absence of stereotypes in these episodes underscores the racial segregation of contemporary film roles, since these cartoons suggest that a black figure exhibiting generalized racial traits would not have been a convincing pilot or war hero.

The favorable response from viewers to the "Looney Tunes" series inspired the distributor to explore further possibilities in song exploitation via the cartoon medium. In 1931 Harman-Ising began producing the "Merrie Melodies" cartoons, which consisted of a chain of gags and, for the centerpiece, a Warner tune. The studio made the decision to feature different protagonists in every episode of its new series; thus Bosko remained Harman-Ising's major breadwinner. The distributor continued to finance the production of cartoons for three decades after Harman and Ising went to MGM in 1933 and took their blackface sprite with them. Nevertheless, the fact remains that Warner Brothers' long association with animation started with an African American male figure.

Like Harman-Ising's "Looney Tunes" episodes starring Bosko, the 1930 "Aesop's Fables" cartoon *Dixie Days* from producer Amadee Van Beuren also toyed with conventional ethnic imagery. The film added a new twist to animated black representation by using both minstrel songs and jazz to accompany depictions of African American characters as animal figures. *Dixie Days* followed the lead of nineteenth-century minstrel shows in turning Harriet Beecher Stowe's famous abolition-themed novel *Uncle Tom's Cabin* (1852) into a comical, nostalgic look at the antebellum South. The cartoon also borrowed from the feature films *Hallelujah!* and *Hearts in Dixie*, both of which had pioneered the association of the musical genre with African American plantation life. The studio did not choose a specific animal to represent each ethnic group; both the protagonist slave Uncle Tom and the evil master Simon Legree appear as dogs, and they have similar blackface-influenced features. Only the songs accompanying each character's scenes and some of their actions distinguish them from one another ethnically.[4]

Dixie Days significantly altered the abolitionist sentiment of the book to present the message that slaves accepted, even liked, the "peculiar institution," just not their cruel owners. The film completely ignores the author's runaway slave character George, and the female slave Eliza no longer flees from a plantation but rather from the malicious Legree. Her escape across blocks of ice floating on a body of water remains in the film because the animators could create gags out of the scene, such as having Eliza hop to the rhythm of the music score. Also, the novel's religious references, which had served to enhance the author's abolitionist views, disappear on film. Uncle Tom does not exhibit religious piety, display any biblical knowledge, or utter lines such as "The Lord may help me, or not help; but I'll hold to him, and believe him to the last!" Finally, in the novel Legree kills Tom because the slave worships God, not the owner. In the animation the slave kills Legree; he does not become a martyred Christian.[5]

For *Dixie Days,* the animators constructed broad visual racial stereotypes that contributed to the representations of African Americans as animals. These images, which came from popular culture, distinguished the slave animals from the free (white) ones. The slave animals, mostly dogs, wear ragged clothes and lazily pick cotton. Recalling the metamorphosis gags of the silent era, a watermelon transforms into a close-up image of a whistling slave's face. Some images are even less subtle, as in the scene in which a group of chained slaves skip along happily singing while holding a sign that reads "Slave auction today."

There were not as many verbal stereotypes available from which to construct slave figures as visual ones. Owing to the reluctance of illustrators to animate to dialogue in the early sound cartons, their images of slaves contrast with representations of African Americans in live-action movies of the early 1930s. *Dixie Days* was one of very few films made before 1950 that featured slave characters speaking formal English instead of the dialect usually given to African American characters in film and literature. Words like "dese" (these) and "dem" (them) and the malapropism "regusted" (disgusted) do not appear in Van Beuren's cartoon. Because animators struggled to draw the movement of a figure's mouth accurately, unintelligibly pronounced "Negro dialect" would have been an especially formidable challenge to them. The only animated dialogue in *Dixie Days* comes from Uncle Tom's slowly enunciated line "Hello, Topsy. Where's Little Eva?" As an abstract means of constructing slaves, his utterance is a perfect verbal complement to the animal designs of Uncle Tom, Eliza, and Topsy.

Van Beuren's music director Gene Rodemich gave minstrel tunes the function of musically representing the pre–Civil War South as a happy period for slaves. Every song he chose contained lyrics expressing an ex-slave's longing to return home to his old plantation and his former owner. The opening scene of *Dixie Days* features slaves singing "Carry Me Back to Old Virginny." Toward the middle of the film, Uncle Tom and the slave girl Topsy (depicted as a monkey) dance to Stephen Foster's "Old Folks at Home." As "Old Black Joe" plays in the episode's climax, Tom kills Legree in order to keep him from catching Eliza. Finally, the picture ends with the slaves singing a chorus of Dan Emmett's wistful "Dixie."

While songs derived from minstrelsy augment the portrayal of slaves as content on the plantation, jazz music accompanies scenes depicting slaves' sadness. By using jazz in this manner, Rodemich gave slave figures an emotional complexity that deviated from the characterization of African Americans in other contemporary animations as well as live-action films. The sorrowful jazz scenes do not contradict the film's images of happy slaves; rather, jazz plays as the slaves reluctantly leave the plantation to be sold on the auction block. Thus, jazz actually shares minstrelsy's role in musically emphasizing the slave's fondness for the master's plantation. Rodemich borrowed African American composer W. C. Handy's 1914 song "St. Louis Blues" for a scene in which Tom and Topsy glumly dance on an auction block, dreading their sale. Though written more than six decades after Stowe's book first appeared, "St. Louis Blues" contains lyrics that speak to the feelings of the slave characters. The line "I hate to see de ev'nin' sun go down / Cause my baby, he done lef dis town" corresponds with the desire of Tom and Topsy not to be separated from the loved ones of their slave community. "I'll pack my trunk / Make ma get away," meanwhile, foreshadows Eliza's getaway from Legree. Rodemich could have picked other tunes by composers of other ethnic groups to express musically the despondency of the slaves. For this reason his choice of a blues song by an African American composer especially underscores the black identity of the animal slaves.[6]

The success of *Dixie Days* gave rise to more cartoons that featured emotionally complex slaves. In April 1930 *Exhibitors' Herald-World* reported, "Loew's circuit has signed 'Dixie Days,' latest Pathé Aesop Sound Fable, for 180 days in New York and Brooklyn, breaking the record of 158 days of 'Good Old School Days.'" Van Beuren's competitors produced parodies of *Uncle Tom's Cabin* that similarly used minstrel songs to show slavery in a positive light and jazz to depict the sadness of slaves. The Warner Brothers cartoon *Hittin' the Trail to Hallelujahland* (1931) features Tom—essentially Bosko with a gray beard—singing the minstrel song "De Camptown Ladies" while driving a stagecoach. He then wanders into a graveyard, where he cowers at the sight of living skeletons singing a jazzy song.[7]

Max Fleischer, now making cartoons for Paramount Pictures, also produced a few films starring slave characters and synchronized them to minstrel songs. His "Screen Song" series features contemporary popular ballads and old folksongs. In each episode numerous characters perform gags related to the featured song. The "Screen Songs," as a result, resemble the blackface minstrel shows in structure—a hodgepodge of musical numbers and random jokes appearing in rapid succession. One film, *Old Black Joe,* features gags about slavery and the song for which the cartoon is named. The film *Sweet Jennie Lee* presents more antebellum humor and includes "Dixie" as background music. These tributes to the "peculiar institution" were rare, however. The studio was better known for its illustrations of urban life in the context of African American jazz.[8]

Although many of Fleischer's animators shared the Disney studio's embrace of African American jazz, the Fleischer cartoons promoting this music developed completely different images to correspond to the featured songs. Contrasting with Disney's Kansas-inspired images of carefree rural animals, Fleischer's New York–based films usually starred characters either enjoying or suffering from urban life. Their actions ranged from gambling and, for male characters, propositioning women to dancing to jazz. Like the Disney films, however, Fleischer's cartoons reflected the en-

vironment and lifestyles of their animators; animator Shamus Culhane recalled his Fleischer Studio colleagues' weekly sexual encounters, alcoholic
binges, and card games with prostitutes in the early 1930s.[9]

Fleischer's "Talkartoon" episode *Ace of Spades* (1930) was of the first
cartoons to associate African American music with urban characters.
The studio initially produced sound-synchronized films by animating to
phonograph records and making the figures move superfluously to every
musical beat. The soundtrack to *Ace of Spades,* which consists entirely
of a recorded performance by black vaudevillians, accompanies the adventures of a character with a gambling habit. This urban "card shark"
with an African American voice was unique among representations of the
ethnic group in cartoons because he relied on himself for survival. He
was neither, like Sammy Johnsin, a helpless, juvenile sambo living with
his mother nor a carefree slave skipping on a plantation, as in *Dixie Days.*
Ace of Spades does, however, introduce a new racial stereotype: it presents
blacks as poor urbanites seeking a quick way to earn money but glosses
over the root causes of urban poverty such as discrimination in labor and
in education.[10]

Not only did "race records" serve as accompaniment to cartoons, but
also the cartoons were produced in a manner that resembled a jazz performance. Culhane, despite acknowledging an aversion to jazz in his auto-
biography, likens the production process to a jam session, in which individual players take turns improvising on a melody. Each animator of a film
would improvise on a script's theme by creating his own camera shots,
gags, and supporting characters but would not deviate too far from the
story so as to keep his scenes compatible with those of the other animators.
Director Dave Fleischer would suggest improvised, unscripted jokes for
his animators to incorporate in a cartoon.[11]

The character Bimbo the Dog often functioned as Fleischer's animated
representation of the African American jazz artist and starred in many of
the cartoons featuring that music genre. His appearance varied from film
to film; some animators drew him as a white dog, while others made him
jet black like Mickey Mouse and Felix the Cat. Despite the jazz music that
illustrated his adventures, the studio did not promote Bimbo as an African
American character. Former Fleischer animator Myron Waldman makes
the important point that "all the early animation until the early '30s was

done in black and white and shades of gray—giving the impression that Bimbo might have been a black face character. I don't think this was the case in Bimbo—[in] either drawing or voice."[12]

The studio's 1930 "Talkartoon" episode *Hot Dog* demonstrates Bimbo's talent for cultural appropriation. The film synchronizes the character's movement to a phonograph record as Bimbo pantomimes the white banjoist Eddie Peabody's performance of Handy's "St. Louis Blues." Bimbo's singing of Handy's work in Peabody's voice parallels Fleischer's role as a modern-day minstrel—a white animation producer creating animated films, cartoon characters, and gags based on African American music.

Audiences responded favorably to the African American sounds of Fleischer's cartoons. Critics often paid more attention to the studio's musical selection for a cartoon than to the visual content of the film itself. The studio, however, did not make films with strong plots, and Bimbo's variable design demonstrates what animator Culhane refers to as the studio's lack of commitment to characterization. Reviewing the Fleischer cartoon *Hot Dog*, a critic for *Variety* praised a scene in which Bimbo performs Handy's song: "Court scene, where dog is playing 'St. Louis Blues' on a banjo, was feminine 'blues' voice and strumming, and it possesses a real 'hot' quality." The periodical published another review that praised the African American sounds of the studio's *Ace of Spades*: "Perfect synchronization with pantomime and action, plus nice set-up of special songs of the Negro spiritual type, effectively sung, set this cartoon apart from the run, and, together with general workmanship in other respects, gives it better than average rating. Spottable on any bill anywhere. Animal character is Bombo, cat, who's a card sharp, and most of the action centers around a poker game. The special songs are written to the tune of well-known spirituals."[13]

Despite the innovations by Van Beuren and Fleischer, as late as 1931 some studios were still having trouble using sound to enhance black characterization. That year a *Variety* reviewer discussed the recently released cartoon *Blues* from Paul Terry's new Terrytoons studio in New York, calling it "a disjointed story of a colored hobo and his mule who tempts a mammy with his music and they wed. On the return from the ceremony he pipes her basketful of kids and lams out." This critic was one of the first to note that a cartoon's African American characters did not sound black.

Blues, the critic wrote, "has one pointed angle in that all the characters are black face, although offscreen singing voices sound otherwise." The writer expected the characters to speak in the exaggerated manner of blackface minstrels, which he considered essential to African American characterization. Moreover, he attests to the American public's acceptance of exaggerated racial caricatures in African American representation by interchangeably referring to the characters as "colored" and "black face."[14]

In 1932 studios began searching for new ways to combine sound with animation. Musicals starring nondescript characters had run their course; this was the year when Max Fleischer, for example, stopped producing his "Talkartoons." Sound synchronization was no longer a novelty. Most cartoon series still promoted songs, especially music owned by the series' distributors, but the characters talked at greater length in between the featured songs. Changes in viewers' tastes forced animators to become as adept at animating to dialogue as to music.

Some critics of animated films, however, still preferred cartoon musicals to talking characters. They felt that the animating dialogue did not work. Combining music and drawn figures was one thing, but simulating the spoken word was quite another. A critic for *Variety* lamented that Ub Iwerks's cartoon *The Cuckoo Murder Case* "is making the mistake of having the figures talk." Gilbert Seldes similarly complained in 1932: "I think because Mickey Mouse is a character, Disney finds himself forced occasionally to endow him with a verbal wit and to give him too much to say, which is against the spirit of the animated cartoon. The great satisfaction in the first animated cartoons was that they used sound properly—the sound was as unreal as the action; the eye and the ear were not at war with each other, one observing a fantasy, the other an actuality. The words of Mickey Mouse are still disguised as animal sounds, but the moment they are recognizable the perfection of animated drawing is corrupted."[15]

Critics notwithstanding, Van Beuren spent the next two years (1932–34) developing verbal humor instead of visual humor, and he drew from African American caricature to shape it. Because his films from this period were among the first to rely principally on dialogue for humor, African Americans indirectly contributed to the breaking of additional new ground in sound-synchronized animation. Some cartoons consisted almost entirely of black and blackfaced characters telling jokes to one another. The "Tom and Jerry" cartoon *Plane Dumb* (1932) and the "Amos 'n' Andy" animated series demonstrated the importance of "Negro dialect" to American animation's shift in synchronization from music to dialogue.

In *Plane Dumb* makes no attempt to hide its intention to exploit for profit the presumed intrinsic humor of African American speech. The film consists merely of seven minutes of blackface minstrel repartee. The convoluted plot concerns white explorers Tom and Jerry, who blacken their faces in order to look like Africans. They reason that by doing so, they can avoid being attacked by the inhabitants of the continent. The pair do not dress in the stereotypical grass skirts or wear bones in their hair but rather retain their jackets, slacks, and ties, and they disguise their voices by speaking in the usual manner of African American characters instead of mimicking an African language. Finally, the characters do not even encounter Africans until the last minute of the cartoon. At that point Tom and Jerry run from the indigenous Africans' bows and spears without a word, thus rendering irrelevant the entire premise of blacking up and caricaturing African American speech to fool Africans.

A reviewer for *Variety* who dismissed *Plane Dumb* as suitable for only the "medium class houses and lesser spots" provides a stark contrast to the plethora of commentators in diverse periodicals—from *Time* to the *New Republic*—who praised the early Mickey Mouse cartoons (1928–1931) featuring minstrel songs. The derogation of *Plane Dumb* as unappealing to the elite recalls the initial disdain of the wealthy classes in the nineteenth century for the stage performances of working-class immigrants in blackface. The "Mickey Mouse" films drew their humor primarily from visual gags, unlike *Plane Dumb*'s reliance on the comic banter between Tom and Jerry. To be sure, the reviewer considered the cartoon's use of dialogue a key factor in drawing audiences: "The synchronization is okay and contains some vocalizing besides the usual bone rattling episodes of skeleton figures." Nevertheless, according to the reviewer, the voices and the characters' lines did not enhance the characterization of the animated stars. A greater problem was that Van Beuren's stars apparently needed the help of blackface humor to draw laughs from audiences, implying that Tom and Jerry were not funny as themselves but only in disguise.[16]

Despite the lukewarm reception received by *Plane Dumb* in theaters, Van Beuren still hoped that the use of authentic blackface minstrelsy in animated cartoons would reverse the studio's declining fortunes. Having dropped the "Aesop's Fables" and "Tom and Jerry" series in 1933, the studio suffered the failure later that year of its newest series, "Cubby Bear," which starred a bear resembling Mickey Mouse. But Van Beuren struck gold when Freeman Gosden and Charles Correll, white actors who voiced the African American characters Amos Jones and Andrew H. Brown in their long-running radio program *Amos 'n' Andy* (1925–60), agreed to lend their voices and characters to Van Beuren for an animated adaptation. Like their radio counterparts, the animated Amos, Andy, and other African American characters in the series spoke in "Negro dialect," and Van Beuren wasted no opportunity to exploit the voices that were familiar to millions of listeners.

Despite the input of Gosden and Correll, the "Amos 'n' Andy" cartoons were fundamentally different from the radio episodes. For example, the radio show had included female love interests for Amos and Andy, but the cartoons did not. Although many cartoons starred male-female couples such as Mickey and Minnie Mouse, cartoons featuring heterosexual black couples were extremely rare. By deleting the characters' girlfriends, the studio followed the standard practice in Hollywood of keeping African American male characters asexual. Also, unlike the continuing half-hour daily adventures of the original show, the animated stories were formulaic, self-contained six-minute short films. In each cartoon Andy's lodge brother Kingfish would persuade him to participate in a "get rich quick" scheme despite Amos's protests.

The "Amos 'n' Andy" cartoons offered some original and progressive aspects of African American characterization. The characters lived in a modern urban environment, whereas earlier African American cartoon figures tended to live in rural settings. As a result, they were the first animated depiction of the "Zip Coon" character type (an ignorant African American Northerner), cartoon symbol of the contemporary phenomenon of African Americans' urban migration from Southern farmlands to Northern cities. More important, they were among the very few animated African American characters who owned their own businesses. The scenes in the cartoons showing Amos and Andy working at their taxicab company gave recognition to the rarely publicized majority of Harlemites who worked for a living. Downtown Harlem's late-night partygoers—later caricatured as crapshooters and jitterbugs in movies and cartoons set in the city— constituted less than 10 percent of the community. Van Beuren thus presented unique and sensitive characterizations by showing urban African Americans at work during the Great Depression.[17]

"Amos 'n' Andy" broke new ground in other important areas. It was the first cartoon series since the silent era to star African American protagonists as opposed to racially inflected anthropomorphic animals. More than that, it was one of the first series to feature black characters exclusively; there were no white or animal characters even in cameo roles. The series also differed from most of its counterparts in that it neither featured a song nor required Amos and Andy to sing and dance. As nonmusical African Americans, Gosden's and Correll's characters were highly unusually.

The series also provided original designs for black figures. The animated Amos Jones and Andy Brown were two of the first African American characters whose appearance broke out of the "Felix the Cat" mold. Instead of jet-black skin, both are drawn in tones of light gray. They have broad noses with delineated nostrils, and their lips are smaller than in African American cartoon caricatures, though still prominent. In one advertisement the studio promised that Amos and Andy would look "just as their millions of radio fans imagine them." To accomplish this goal, animators tried to make the characters realistically human. As animator Bill Littlejohn recalled: "There was nothing exaggerated or caricatured about the drawings of the faces. They were pretty much drawn to scale." He also remembered rotoscoping the characters—animating the figures by tracing the movements of people from frames of live-action film.[18]

The studio's "Amos 'n' Andy" series marked the final collaboration of Gosden and Correll with Van Beuren's distributor, Radio-Keith-Orpheum (RKO). *Check and Double Check* (1930), a feature film starring the actors in blackface in their radio roles, had not met with the financial success envisioned by RKO, which had invested heavily in the picture. Like the cartoons, the movie also had jettisoned the female characters; nor did the backdrops reflect the radio show's Harlem setting. Van Beuren's series, however, had an advantage over *Check and Double Check*. Whereas the feature problematically had tried to convince audiences that under the burnt cork Gosden and Correll corresponded to radio listeners' mental images of

Amos and Andy, Van Beuren's animated images of the characters approximated real African Americans. They weren't simply drawings of Gosden and Correll in blackface.[19]

The dialogue of the "Amos 'n' Andy" cartoons was both the main attraction of the series and its tragic flaw. When advertising the series, the studio concentrated more on the familiarity of the voices than on the quality of the animation. A trade advertisement heralding the arrival of Amos and Andy "with their own voices in animated cartoons" provided an example of the type of "Negro" speech audiences should expect: "'Undisconnected wid de Fresh Air Taxicab Co. of America, Incorpulated,' Andrew H. Brown, President, Andrew H. Brown, Director, Andrew H. Brown, Author, Andrew H. Brown, Cameraman and Amos Jones, Property Man, announce the first super-supreme-colossal-de luxe production of 'The Great Animater Pitcher Co. of America, Incorpulated' Entitled 'The Rasslin' Match.'" Exhibitors generally lauded the cartoon characters for using the same voices as their radio counterparts. J. J. Medford noted, "Amos and Andy do the talking and just like the radio." A. N. Miles similarly noted, "The voices are natural and drawing is good." The verbal humor of radio's *Amos 'n' Andy*, however, did not adapt successfully to animation. The cartoons relied on dialogue at the expense of action; characters often stopped moving while they spoke. Medford, despite calling *The Rasslin' Match* "one of the best cartoons I have ever seen," complained, "There is only one mistake, the cartoon is entirely too crude."[20]

The dialogue served as a crutch for animators who were almost completely unfamiliar with the task of developing funny gags for human characters. For the past fifteen years, the Van Beuren Studio had rarely produced a cartoon that did not feature a leading or secondary animal character. In taking on "Amos 'n' Andy," the animators were suddenly working exclusively on animating people. But their concentration on making the characters look realistically African American meant that the studio's usual surreal gags—like the watermelon-to-slave dog's face in *Dixie Days*—would be out of place. The two main visual jokes in *The Rasslin' Match* involve Andy's literally turning white with fright and the boxer Mooseface's countenance transforming from its African American features to the face of a moose. Apart from these few gags, the cartoonists relied on Gosden and Correll's verbal exchanges to fill the void in visual humor.

Van Beuren's "Amos 'n' Andy" was an expensive series to produce. Bill Littlejohn noted, "It took a lot of drawing to make these characters—the buttons and other details." The complex, realistic animation required more celluloid sheets than usual. The dominance of verbal humor meant an increase in the use of tape for recording voices. In addition, the episodes ran longer than previous cartoons from the "Aesop's Fables" and "Tom and Jerry" series. Van Beuren's investment in "Amos 'n' Andy" was unprecedented in American animation; no cartoon producer had previously gambled so heavily on familiar African American characterizations to score with audiences. The stakes were especially high for Van Beuren, who needed a new hit series.[21]

The animated "Amos 'n' Andy" was not a success. RKO Radio Pictures released only two cartoons—*The Rasslin' Match* and *The Lion Tamer*—before replacing the series with the fairy-tale stories of the "Rainbow Parade" cartoons by year's end. This new direction spelled the end of the studio's reliance on verbal blackface minstrelsy. Littlejohn considered the "Amos 'n' Andy" stories "the weak part [of the studio's cartoon output]." Many early live-action sound films, released in the late 1920s, were essentially filmed plays saturated with dialogue; these movies failed to score with audiences because of their lack of visual excitement. The "Amos 'n' Andy" cartoons therefore represented a step backward in filmmaking since they were essentially filmed radio programs.[22]

Although Max Fleischer shared Van Beuren's tactic of appropriating African American speech in animation, Fleischer preferred more contemporary jazz performers to blackface minstrels. By 1932 his studio no longer synchronized cartoons to "race records" but rather arranged for the musicians to voice characters and sing for the films. Studio employees visited jazz clubs in New York and chose the acts they wanted for the cartoons. If a musician agreed to star in and sing for a cartoon, Paramount Pictures would promise to release the film to the theater where he was scheduled to appear. Former Fleischer animator Myron Waldman remembered, "The performers jumped at the chance to appear on screens all over—coverage they could not get before."[23]

Like Harman-Ising's films, Fleischer's cartoons were little more than animated jazz performances. Writers constructed cartoon stories loosely based on the songs they had heard the musicians play in the clubs.

Animators then filmed the singers' movements and rotoscoped the frames to create cartoon figures. The Fleischer studio's focus on the singer was what differentiated its cartoons from the song-focused "Looney Tunes" and "Merrie Melodies."[24]

Fleischer also differed from Harman-Ising by using African American music to present a brand-new style of humor to film audiences. Dave Fleischer, Max's brother and the director of his films, favored the "New Humor" of New York's vaudeville entertainers. This style corresponded to the Fleischer brothers' sensibility in relation to their first-generation Austrian American ethnicity. The "New Humorists" made jokes about immigration and spoofed European dialects. They broke from American minstrelsy by delivering jokes as quick one-liners in comparison to minstrels' long "stump" speeches. In addition, a common theme of "New Humor" performance was the rube in the big city. In several Fleischer cartoons, white characters leave the shelter of their homes to visit the exciting but dangerous environments of the characters played by black musicians. The 1932 "Talkartoon" film *Minnie the Moocher* casts Betty Boop as a runaway escaping her strict, heavy-accented Jewish immigrant father for a frightening cave haunted by ghosts who sound like Cab Calloway and his orchestra.[25]

Before the Fleischers, no cartoon producer had developed characters based on real African Americans. The Fleischers cast certain black musicians in films because of their popularity with white audiences. The studio incorporated African American performance into its films in a similar manner to blackface minstrels' incorporation of black dance and speech into their acts decades earlier. Just as minstrels had studied African Americans in taverns and dancehalls, at festivals, and on visits to plantations, Lou Fleischer—Max's brother—visited Harlem's Cotton Club to see Calloway's nightclub act. Calloway's unique dance steps and singing style appealed to the filmmakers and also to audiences, who generated enough demand that Fleischer produced four cartoons starring Calloway. In contrast, Louis Armstrong's act lacked the visual appeal of Calloway's dances, so the studio integrated more live-action footage than rotoscoped animation into Armstrong's only cartoon, *I'll Be Glad When You're Dead You Rascal You* (1932). The animators depicted him as merely a floating, disembodied head singing the title song as Betty Boop and Koko the Clown ran from him. One exhibitor consequently praised the tune more than the cartoon: "The music is furnished by Louis Armstrong and his band and it will make a good filler on any program. The cartoon is also good, but the orchestra will prove the best business getter."[26]

The studio's films starring these artists are significant artifacts of African American performance during the Harlem Renaissance of the 1920s and early 1930s. The Fleischers were among a number of white people promoting urban African American artists and writers who deliberately avoided using minstrelsy-derived imagery for their work. Instead, these artists developed their own ethnic representations. For example, the jazz musicians in clubs patronized by the Fleischers wore formal suits instead of oversized, clownish costumes, and they sang in the urban black vernacular instead of "Negro dialect." As the depression spread in the early thirties and Harlem slowly evolved into a slum whose residents suffered from declining incomes and massive unemployment, the area's late-night entertainment scene became less appealing to patrons, and it too began to decline. The Fleischer studio's cartoons recorded the last gasp of the Harlem Renaissance.[27]

The Fleischers also broke new ground in animated African American representation by presenting characters engaged in interracial sexual innuendo. Such content was taboo at a time of racial segregation in the United States. Even in live-action films, black musicians played in nightclub settings on stages far from white spectators and did not interact with white female characters. By contrast, the Fleischers usually cast African American entertainers as lustful brutes in pursuit of their major cartoon star, Betty Boop—a young, "flapperish" white woman—in the "Talkartoons" and "Betty Boop" series. In several cartoons Betty teases male figures by singing sexually suggestive lyrics to songs but flees when they stop flirting and try to overpower her physically. This formula accounts for the majority of the episodes featuring black music or animated representations of jazz artists. Calloway's ghost caricature in *Minnie the Moocher* sings about the title character, "She was a red-hot hoochie-coocher," and his cave-dwelling hermit character in *The Old Man of the Mountain* fondles Betty Boop's breasts and waist.[28]

The Old Man of the Mountain (1933), a "Betty Boop" cartoon, uses contrasting backgrounds to depict interracial sex as "forbidden fruit."

Although Betty shares screen space with non-servile black characters, she and her black co-stars do not live in the same community. Betty's neighborhood is safe, while the cave in which Calloway's hermit character lives is forbidding. The ghosts and cannibals played by black entertainers in Fleischer films live only among other ghosts and cannibals, thus suggesting an ethnically specific environment. In the opening scenes of *The Old Man of the Mountain*, the desperate escapes of various animal characters from the hermit's cave reflect the abandonment by whites of neighborhoods inhabited by blacks. Betty always leaves these environments once she gets sufficient exposure to the jazz and dancing of the black entertainers. These African American performers and the surreal dwellings of their caricatures in the "Betty Boop" series represent an "other" that provides an appealing sense of liberation for whites but contains a threat of miscegenation via Betty's presence in their part of town. *The Old Man of the Mountain* illustrates this danger with a gag in which a distraught female fugitive from the cave pushes a carriage full of babies resembling the hermit.[29]

To be sure, characters inspired by African Americans are not Betty's only pursuers. As the film historian Jake Austen points out, plenty of white and animal characters also express their physical attraction to Betty. Indeed, white employers in *Boop-Oop-A-Doop* and *Betty Boop's Big Boss* proposition her at work. Austen also notes that audiences of the 1930s did not express any consciousness of interracial relationships. Their silence on the matter does not mean, however, that the message was not present. In addition, Austen neglects to mention that the Fleischer studio also cast white characters such as Koko the Clown and a muscular man named Freddie as heroes who rescue Betty but did not provide any images other than the lustful pursuers for black artists to perform. As a result, African American music and suggestive content became inextricably linked in the "Betty Boop" series.[30]

The Fleischer staff took great care in animating images to Calloway's songs in *The Old Man of the Mountain*. Although the animators rotoscoped the performer's dance steps for the "Old Man" character, they also added touches of characterization to the "Old Man" himself; the hermit displays bowed legs and crossed eyes while perfectly reproducing Calloway's moves. The artists expertly animated the hermit's lip movements to the entertainer's scat singing—a remarkable feat, considering the rapid-fire procession of consonants that Calloway uttered when vocalizing in this fashion. Moreover, rotoscoping and animating so much dialogue were expensive techniques, thus demonstrating the tremendous faith that Paramount Pictures and Fleischer had in Calloway's popularity with audiences.

The studio demonstrated its fondness for Calloway's showmanship by having his character in *The Old Man of the Mountain* interact with Betty Boop. In Fleischer's previous black jazz musicals *Minnie the Moocher*, *I'll Be Glad When You're Dead You Racsal You*, and *Snow White*, the characters played by the vocalists sing to Betty Boop and her cohorts. *The Old Man of the Mountain*, however, features a duet between Calloway and Mae Questel, the voice of Betty Boop. Also, the musician has a line of spoken dialogue—a rarity for an African American actor in cartoons of the early and mid-1930s. He responds to Betty's question "What'cha gonna do now?" with "Gonna do the best I can."

The animators of these particular cartoons considered their work a labor of love. They were able to choose which films to work on. Whereas Shamus Culhane avoided animating to Calloway's songs because the illustrator did not appreciate the music, Willard Bowsky animated some of the films precisely because of his fondness for jazz. Berny Wolf, another Fleischer animator, recalled having heard Calloway perform during the production of *The Old Man of the Mountain* and having liked his music. Wolf found Calloway "an enjoyable personality" to animate. The animators developed humor from Calloway's singing style by making the hermit character's cries of pain coincide with the singer's shouts during his songs. According to Fleischer historian Leslie Cabarga, Calloway himself found his animated likenesses amusing.[31]

The Old Man of the Mountain was one of many films—live action and animated—that some Americans at the time, especially Catholics, considered controversial. In Fleischer's cartoons Betty Boop wears a short dress and a garter belt while she sings her suggestive songs. Exhibitors began to complain about the mature content of "Boop" cartoons in the mid-1930s. One theater owner worried especially about the impact of *The Old Man of the Mountain*'s sex and jazz on juvenile audiences. "After being an enthusiast on these Screen Songs it was an awful let-down to have to show this reel," he remarked. "It seems to me that there is but little excuse to take a cartoon that is primarily the one thing in the show the kids really like and make it a vulgar, smutty blare of noise and gags without humor."[32]

In response to the complaints, Paramount Pictures, Fleischer's distributor, warned the studio to tone Betty down. The animators obliged, thus rendering the jazzmen and their music obsolete. The studio dropped the suggestive songs, lecherous friends like Bimbo Dog, and stories involving Betty fighting off lustful men. In dispensing with the African American entertainers and their music after limiting the "Betty Boop" series' sexual references, Fleischer thus acknowledged the widely assumed connection between raciness and blackness. Betty's dresses now stopped at her knees rather than her thighs. The studio set many of the later "Betty Boop" cartoons in Betty's home, a domesticity that was not congruent with the sexual themes of the earlier cartoons. Betty encounters the predatory characters with African American voices only after she leaves the comfort of her home. In contrast, friendlier and less controversial co-stars such as the jovial Grampy and the cute but feisty Pudgy Pup come to her home. She now sings "I've Got Those Housecleaning Blues" while confined to her all-white neighborhood, away from the "dangerous" black environments where figures sing about "red-hot hoochie-coochers."[33]

The backlash against "Betty Boop" had as much to do with her black co-stars as with the musical selections and the length of her dresses. The urban characters voiced by blacks are fundamentally different from the more typical animated Southern black figures of the day. While both kinds of characters are musical and carefree, the Southern characters have a restricted social "place" and defer to whites; the Northern jazz figures, in contrast, defer to nobody. Whereas the peppy, bouncy energy of slave figures appears solely in relation to their plantation work for white owners, the "free," urban, lecherous characters use that same energy to express themselves sexually to white women. From the mid-1930s onward, Fleischer banned African American sexual expression from his films; no black character of any kind would ever romance or dance closely with Betty Boop for the remainder of the series.

The disappearance of black jazz from Fleischer's cartoons coincided with the end of the Harlem Renaissance. Many years later, when asked why the studio had stopped using jazz entertainers, former animator Myron Waldman recalled: "The formula was changed. Betty had the little pup

Pudgy. Besides, I think like all cycles, the demand for that type of vocals dropped in the marketplace." But more than that, several social factors were involved. By 1934 half of Harlem's families were unemployed, and fewer than 10 percent of them would receive government-relief jobs in the later 1930s. Tuberculosis, syphilis, and pneumonia afflicted Harlemites to a much greater degree than other Manhattan residents. In 1935 ten thousand Harlem residents rioted. Even if the Hays Code had not altered Betty, the Fleischers would not have been able to "sell" the old images of the nightlife as easily as they had before. After *Betty Boop's Rise to Fame* (1934), a cartoon containing footage of *The Old Man of the Mountain*, African American jazz musicians never starred in another Fleischer film.[34]

The Van Beuren and Fleischer studios found that black representation had its limits of acceptance with white audiences. Jazz had inspired animators to extend black imagery beyond the South. In doing so, however, some artists illustrated black-white relationships outside the context of white dominance in a manner that tested the tolerance of many viewers. Consequently, animators spent the next few years developing stories and characterizations that would avoid arousing the disapproval of exhibitors and religious leaders. As we will see in the next chapter, that process largely involved returning to the Southern black characterizations audiences had long favored.

THREE

Black Characterizations

IN 1930 THE Motion Picture Producers and Distributors Association (MPPDA) enacted the Motion Picture Production Code (henceforth the Code) for filmmakers to follow. Throughout the 1920s civic and religious groups, furious at the increasing sexual and violent content of films, had called for either the movie industry to censor itself or the federal government to institute controls. Code author Martin Quigley, a devout Catholic and the publisher of the trade periodical *Motion Picture Herald*, consulted with Catholic leaders before drafting the new rules. In general terms, the Code sought to affirm the principles of "good taste," requiring that "no picture shall be produced which will lower the standards of those who see it." It stipulated that "the sympathy of the audience should never be thrown on the side of crime, wrongdoing, evil or sin," that "revenge . . . shall not be justified," and that "the sanctity of the institution of marriage and the home shall be upheld." Specific rules prohibited profanity, including "the words God, Lord, Jesus, Christ—unless used reverently," as well as the portrayal of ministers of religion "as comic characters or as villains." Also forbidden was the depiction of "excessive and lustful kissing," "suggestive postures and gestures," and any hint of "sex relationships between the black and white races."[1]

During the 1930s, as we have seen, most of these rules were honored mainly in the breach. As movie attendance dropped with the onset of the Great Depression, Hollywood resorted to the tried-and-true formulas of the past, sex and violence included, in order to attract audiences. In response, religious organizations as well as government officials went back on the attack. Catholic leaders nationwide urged boycotts of objectionable movies and blacklisted them in denominational magazines. In Congress, Raymond Cannon, a Wisconsin Democrat, introduced a bill designed to punish distributors of films involving depravity or containing mature and morally offensive content.[2]

By 1934 the film industry decided that it could no longer ignore its critics. Under the direction of Will Hays, the MPPDA set up the Production
Code Administration (PCA), an agency composed of executives experienced in handling the MPPDA's relations with movie studios. Hays ap-
pointed Joseph Breen, a Catholic, as the head of the PCA. The MPPDA
ordered its studios to submit scripts to Breen for approval, levied fines
against Code violators, and prohibited the exhibition of films lacking the
Production Code Seal of Approval in its theaters. The PCA began enforc-
ing the Code on July 1, 1934.

After that date, Hollywood began producing completely different kinds
of motion pictures. Gone were the Western and the gangster films, both of
which involved numerous scenes of now taboo gunfights. Another casualty
was Mae West, famous for her portrayals of sexually aggressive women; the
PCA deemed her sexually charged comedies unacceptable, and her career
subsequently went into decline. The new, PCA-approved genres included
screwball comedies, dramas, and musicals. In all of these films, African
Americans played mostly supporting roles as domestic servants or rural
slaves. Animation producers, wanting to keep their contracts with distributors, made corresponding changes to cartoons, discarding the progressive African American images of the early sound era: no more celebrations
of New York jazz, no more black characters owning and operating their
own businesses, no more allusions to interracial sex.[3]

Instead, the servile and passive figures that had been featured in literature for generations accounted for nearly all the African American cartoon characters seen from the Great Depression through World War II.
Such figures were very practical for animators developing PCA-friendly
comedy since they required little characterization; earlier writers had already established their comedic personalities. The images also gave cartoons greater likelihood of success with audiences, for viewers had been
primed through decades' worth of stories to laugh at the characters. They
were in the public domain, so animators did not have to pay licensing fees
to borrow the already popular figures. Moreover, the basic nature of the
characterizations made them easily adaptable to the various story formulas that came and went between the mid-1930s and mid-1940s.

Some studios tried vainly to hold on to jazz celebrities. Co-producers
Hugh Harman and Rudolf Ising, for example, altered black jazz carica-

tures to make them suitable for the Code era. In toning down the famous characterizations, however, Harman-Ising turned the hip, urban Cotton Club musicians into unsophisticated rural blacks. The studio also caricatured them as frogs; former studio animator Mel Shaw recalled that because of their large mouths, frogs were considered suitable animals to depict as African Americans. The amphibious caricatures cavorted in a muddy swamp and, becoming excited by their music, usually ended the cartoons by breaking their instruments. Such imagery was a far cry from the slick, graceful dances rotoscoped by the Fleischers for their jazz figures. Even the music reflected this shift; the studio borrowed Harry Barris's "Mississippi Mud," featuring the racially derisive lyric "Darkies beat your feet," for caricatures of the Mills Brothers to sing in the opening of *Swing Wedding* (1937).[4]

Studio lyricist William Hanna and music director Scott Bradley, the composers of the score for the "jazz-frog" cartoon *The Old Millpond* (1936), wrote music that was significantly less emotionally complex and more generic than that in the pre-Code cartoons —another casualty of African American representation in the aftermath of the PCA's emergence. Calloway's pre-1934 song "Minnie the Moocher" skillfully mixes witty exaggerations like "Each meal she ate was a dozen courses" with lyrics about relationships damaged by drug abuse, such as "She loved-ed him, but he was cokey." In contrast, the lyrics for the frogs have as their themes merely happiness and music itself, displaying neither depth nor humor. In the Hanna-Bradley composition "Preacher Song," a minister joyfully encourages a worshipper, "Smile on, Brother, smile." The song "Jungle Rhythm," written by Hanna alone, offers this testimony on scatting: "So I just give 'em / Jungle Rhythm / Right in style and how / With a bum-ti-de, bum-ti-de, bum / Has changed to Mmm, nah, now."[5]

Even worse, Harman-Ising stripped the black stars of their unique personalities. In contrast to Fleischer's earlier attempts to capture a performer's dance steps, gestures, and expressions, Harman-Ising's animators settled for facial similarity. Even the names of the entertainers mattered little at times. The dialogue continuity sheet for Harman-Ising's cartoon *The Old Millpond* refers anonymously to a caricature of Armstrong as "Fat Frog." Only in the music did the studio attempt accurate characterization. The script for that film has a Calloway caricature singing, "Skit de bot de beet de hi de ho." In *Swing Wedding* one of his lines is "Oww—skippy, itty-uppy / I'm a swing dong daddy / And a hi de hi de hi de hay."[6]

Interestingly, the MGM cartoon *Swing Wedding* exposes the extent to which the PCA selectively enforced the Hays Code. The Code strictly forbade the ridiculing of religion or religious faiths, comical or villainous depictions of ministers, disrespectful images of religious ceremonies, and the words "God" and "Lord" spoken without reverence. *Swing Wedding*, however, flagrantly broke these rules. Harry Barris's song "Mississippi Mud"—the film's opening number—includes the word "Lordy" in its lyrics, which are sung by a preacher during a sermon. The PCA allowed the word to remain, thus permitting a "man of the cloth" to take the Lord's name in vain while theoretically speaking on His behalf. The organization also neglected to censor the preacher's scat singing when he officiates at a wedding: "Is de nay nay nay / Is de no no no / Is dere any doople daddle anna / Is dere any man here who can honestly say / Dat dis here couple can't be wed today." The PCA's authorization of *Swing Wedding*'s scatting preacher and jazz ceremony reveals the group's unwillingness to enforce its own rules where images of African American religious traditions were concerned.[7]

Ironically, *Swing Wedding* violates the Code several times in ways that recall the pre-1934 Fleischer jazz cartoons. This Harman-Ising film is one of very few cartoons that tell the story of an African American love triangle, although the Code forbade such a plot device in a comedy. A Calloway caricature attempts to woo an Ethel Waters frog as she prepares to marry a Stepin' Fetchit frog. Also, the female frogs keep their feet still while swaying their hips—a dance move prohibited by the Code. The Fleischer films often contained both a love triangle and characters dancing suggestively. In the Harman-Ising film, however, all the characters are of color, unlike in the duets between Cab Calloway and Betty Boop. There is no threat of miscegenation, and the songs contain no references to sex and drugs, no "hoochie-coocher" who "kicks the gong around."

These jazz films indicate Harman-Ising's heavy investment in African American caricature. Fifteen of the studio's thirty-five cartoons released by Metro-Goldwyn-Mayer between September 1934 and January 1938 starred African American characters. These were expensive productions—heavily detailed and excessively long. In addition, Harman-Ising took a gamble by spending so much money on films with black characterizations that other studios had avoided in the early years of the Code era. They were too costly, however, and MGM replaced Harman and Ising with new producers, who moved the studio away from depicting black jazz figures.

As with Harman-Ising, Leon Schlesinger Productions also tried to turn jazz figures into PCA-friendly characters. The studio even used the caricatures as tools in preaching morality. Director Friz Freleng's *Clean Pastures* (1937) depicts jazz as both a cause of and a solution for African Americans' urban problems. It differs from the "Betty Boop" series by using jazz music in a rare positive context. In the cartoon, Calloway, Armstrong, and other black entertainers appear as angels luring sinful African Americans from a jazz nightclub to heaven with the brassy song "Swing for Sale." Crowded together atop a bandstand towering above the Harlem streets, the angels are far removed from the people they are trying to save. In addition, their performance of "Swing for Sale" marks one of the few occasions when the lyrics of the featured song of a moral cartoon do not specifically address immoral behavior. The gamblers and nightclub dancers "convert" because of the mere presence of the angels, not the message in their song.

Freleng followed the lead of Harman-Ising in ignoring the intricate details of the celebrities caricatured. *Clean Pastures* offers no approximation of Calloway's dancing, and studio music director Carl Stalling did not try to compose a score that would implement the styles of the artists represented in the film. As in the years when Harman-Ising produced for Warner Brothers, Freleng's cartoon uses none of the songs made famous by the celebrities but rather employs tunes owned by the distributor. Like Harman and Ising, Freleng did not exhibit much knowledge of or sensitivity to the entertainers he caricatured. The script for the film, as approved by him, crudely identifies Calloway's scatting as African American by twice calling for his caricature's "coon shouting."[8]

Clean Pastures was the only cartoon Schlesinger produced that prominently featured a multitude of jazz celebrities. The film was one of the most controversial studio cartoons of the 1930s. The PCA quarreled with producer Schlesinger and distributor Warner Brothers Pictures over the content of the film, a disagreement that resulted in the delay of the cartoon's release by five months. Their correspondence with one another reveals Hollywood's awkward struggle to uphold religious values while placing them in a racially stereotypical context. *Clean Pastures* proved that studios could indeed go too far in lampooning African Americans.[9]

The PCA considered *Clean Pastures* very insensitive to religion. When reviewing the cartoon for approval for release in May 1937, the organization objected to its association of spiritual temptation with both cartoon humor and jazz. The PCA did not want Harold Arlen and E. Y. Harburg's song "Save Me, Sister"—whose lyrics included "Save me from temptation"—as background music for the film's title sequence. The group also objected to the word "Lord" in Peter de Rose and Sam Lewis's song "Half of Me," which appeared in a sequence featuring an African American caricature of Saint Peter. Specifically, the PCA wished to "avoid the impression that the figure approaching the desk is a cartoon of God." On May 11, 1937, Joseph Breen of the PCA wrote to inform Leon Schlesinger that the organization had rejected the film, calling it a "travesty or burlesque on religion, or religious beliefs, honestly maintained."[10]

For the next six months Harry Warner, a co-founder of Warner Brothers Pictures, campaigned vigorously for the PCA's approval of *Clean Pastures*. Although the film was only one of thirty-six cartoons that the distributor released in 1937, *Clean Pastures* had considerable value to its distributor. As one of the Technicolor episodes of the "Merrie Melodies" series, it cost more to produce than any of the black-and-white "Looney Tunes" cartoons. Yet the use of Technicolor made *Clean Pastures* especially attractive to exhibitors, since most cartoons were still not being made in color. In addition, the film stood out from other "Merrie Melodies" entries because it starred caricatures of famous entertainers. Exhibitors preferred booking cartoons that featured popular characters or caricatures, and "Merrie Melodies" episodes usually included neither. Protecting his potentially lucrative film, Warner wrote to Will Hays of the PCA, expressing concern that the studio would face a considerable financial loss with the film's withdrawal. "We have quite a huge investment in Technicolor prints," Warner noted, "and we do not want to hold them up any longer."[11]

Warner did not address the controversy in other than financial terms. He had not participated in the film's development and did not argue about the specific religious issues with the PCA. Moreover, he did not endear himself to the group by belittling its stance. He called the entire controversy "ridiculous," saying, "I don't think that one person of a million would take the view on this subject that the organization has taken." Nevertheless, as a Hollywood executive, he was in a position to influence the PCA, and he utilized that access by appealing to the organization for the film's approval by arranging for the members of the PCA's board of directors to view the cartoon individually and document their reaction to the film.[12]

By early November 1937, Warner Brothers and the PCA had resolved their differences, despite the latter's continued reluctance. The studio agreed to the organization's suggestion to delete the song "Save Me, Sister" and the word "Lord" from "Half of Me." Breen then informed Schlesinger by letter that the PCA had approved the cartoon. When released, the film received a positive response from exhibitors. The sensitivity of Hays and Breen toward religious imagery in films, however, compelled them to disagree with the compromise. They did not like the fact that the nightclub attendees initially ignored the angels and proceeded to gamble and listen to jazz. Hays and Breen also disapproved of the film's use of the song "Oh Dem Golden Slippers." They had noted the previous month that the song was "one of the best known Negro spirituals universally associated in the public mind with religious beliefs of the Negroes." Their only objection, however, was to the use of African American Christian worship music for humorous purposes.[13]

The PCA operated under a double standard concerning ethnic stereotypes as both holy and sinister images. Despite complaints about an African American Saint Peter and the lampooning of worship practices, none of the organization's documents contained any objections to the depiction of Harlem's African Americans as gamblers shooting craps. Also left intact and unnoticed was a scene toward the end in which the jazz angels lead many dancing black couples straight to heaven by playing their music. This image, at best, parodies the biblical concept of the rapture, or the catching up of Christians by Jesus Christ upon His return to earth and, at worst, offers a vision of African American genocide as a solution to urban problems. The PCA even allowed an image of the devil as an African American who enters heaven and enjoys its swing music at the end of the cartoon. In the script Saint Peter assures him, "Sho' dey's always room fo' one mo.'"[14]

The controversy surrounding *Clean Pastures* and the demise of the "jazzy frog" cartoons spelled the end of animation's association with

African American jazz caricatures. From 1938 on such figures appeared very rarely in new cartoons. The entertainers proved too risky of an investment for studios already hampered by the depression. The cartoonists simply stopped trying to soften Armstrong, Calloway, and the others for the PCA.

Animation studios instead sought to lampoon black entertainers who were already acceptable to the PCA. For example, several animators caricatured the African American actor Stepin' Fetchit, a film actor whose exaggerated portrayal of a shuffling, head-scratching, mumbling black man proved immensely popular with white audiences during the late 1920s and early 1930s. From 1927 to 1936 he appeared in an average of three movies a year, typically in the role of a lazy rural laborer always trying to find a way to avoid work. His highly stylized screen persona, reinforced by extravagant off-screen self-promotion, made him ripe for caricature—as himself or as the personification of the generic black male "Jim Crow" characterization.

In Walt Disney's "Silly Symphony" episode *Who Killed Cock Robin* (1935), Fetchit appears as a dimwitted, sleepy-eyed blackbird—one of many birds testifying at a murder trial. Yet if Fetchit's role reinforced the negative stereotype with which he had become associated, the film broke new ground by linking him to white celebrities, who also appear as birds. At the time, producers of feature films were unwilling to risk portraying blacks and whites as peers. In that sense, the film was ahead of its time.

Years after Stepin' Fetchit's career fizzled in the late 1930s, animators still found uses for his characterization of the African American as mentally and physically slow. In the script of MGM's cartoon *The Goose Goes South* (1941) directors William Hanna and Joseph Barbera describe a southern black "tobacco worker" character in a very detailed and redundant manner—"a lazy Stepin' Fetchit type worker listens in a stupid lazy manner"—going to great lengths to establish the character's slothfulness. The script also describes the character's speech as "very slow" and contains unintelligible dialogue for actors to voice for African American characters, reflecting the identification of the characters as rural laborers. Like an auctioneer, one worker chants, "Heh, Bee BB BB BB Blb," and, as the script dictates, "The lazy negro answers the first worker in a very slow manner, 'Ha . . o . . a . . Bl Bl Bl.'"[15]

The Goose Goes South was the latest of films to broadly caricature rural African Americans. Very little changed in the portrayal of animated black rural characters between the mid-1930s and mid-1940s. Instead of setting cartoons in the era of slavery, some studios set their films in the present day and depicted rural blacks as sharecroppers. Nevertheless, the racial stereotypes constituting their visual appearance, speech, and behavior made the time period of each cartoon seem almost superfluous.

Schlesinger Productions used black sharecropper figures for its pioneering "moral cartoon" genre, which blended the African American stereotypes of blackface minstrel shows with religious themes. The episodes reflect the Code's emergence, as characters suddenly receive punishment for committing the same acts that Bosko had gotten away with only two or three years earlier. Many of director Friz Freleng's moral cartoons consist of characters misbehaving, then falling asleep and dreaming of creatures inflicting pain on them as a means of teaching them a lesson, then finally waking and resolving to change their ways. But in Schlesinger's moral cartoons starring black sharecropper caricatures, the protagonists have to learn about the importance of religious faith.

Other distinguishing characteristics of the black moral cartoons involve both the ignorance and the age of the sharecropper figures. To be sure, juvenile animal and white characters appear more often than African American characters as protagonists learning about correct social behavior. Also, black figures occasionally teach the moral lessons, even to characters of other racial groups or species; for example, in the "Looney Tunes" film *Wholly Smoke* (1938), a caricature of Cab Calloway warns Porky Pig not to smoke cigarettes. Nevertheless, black characters learn lessons more often than they teach them. In addition, although the stars of the white moral cartoons are children, the African American figures learning the lessons are usually adults.

While the moral genre was new to animation, it had already appeared in other media. Freleng's first two moral cartoons—*Goin' to Heaven on a Mule* (1934) and *Sunday Go to Meetin' Time* (1936)—had their roots in the popular play and film *The Green Pastures* (1935). Each cartoon borrows from the play's depictions of an African American–populated heaven and hell. The animated characters in need of religion commit such acts as drinking excessively, gambling, and stealing chickens—behavior usually exhibited by black characters in minstrel shows, feature films, and the literature of the day, according to the cultural historian Sterling Brown.[16]

Goin' to Heaven on a Mule, the prototype for Freleng's moral episodes, depicts African Americans in a unique but theologically negative manner. This short tells the story of an alcoholic slave enjoying his inebriety before suffering the consequences in his sleep. The protagonist is one of American animation's first characters to visit hell in his dreams. The film associates his alcoholism with the original sin of the Bible's Adam and Eve by showing a tree of "Forbidden Fruit" full of gin bottles. The cartoon also depicts heaven as "Pair-O-Dice"—a reference not only to "Negro dialect" but also to the stereotype of African Americans as crapshooters. As a Code-era film, this cartoon is a far cry from Harman-Ising's pre-Code "Looney Tunes" film *The Booze Hangs High* (1931), in which several animals become inebriated without suffering consequences.

Freleng's next black moral cartoon—*Sunday Go to Meetin' Time*—features two African American heterosexual couples but, in accordance with the Code's rules about sexual content, does not give their relationships any complexity. The subject of the film is the correction of church truancy. The couples merely serve as means to give structure to the cartoon by performing the main songs and establishing the plot. One couple seems rather dysfunctional, owing to the Code's emphasis on morality. That is, the wife of the African American protagonist behaves more like his mother, dragging him by the ear against his will to church. The African American male adult displays extremely childish behavior. As a result, he resembles an oversized "sambo," sporting a mature physical appearance but behaving just like the silent-era cartoon character Sammy Johnsin. In the film the protagonist runs away from church in order to steal chickens—a plot similar to *Wholly Smoke*'s story of young Porky's truancy from church because of his preference for tobacco. Also, in *Sunday Go to Meetin' Time*, the main character often squats or bends his back, thus shortening his height to that of a child.

Harman-Ising's film *The Old Plantation* (1935) features rural black characters in a dramatic cartoon instead of a moral fantasy. It tells the story of a planter's potential loss of slaves and land because of financial ruin—a situation relevant to suffering Americans during the Great Depression. Furthermore, in depression-era films set in the antebellum South, images of huge mansions surrounded by vast fields symbolized a past time of prosperity in America and the potential to regain that prosperity. Such scenes contrasted with the reality of bread lines, homelessness, and over-crowded cities.[17]

The imagery of slavery in *The Old Plantation* results partly from the new rules of the PCA. The slave figures receive a more humane depiction than in pre-Code cartoons. Unlike the earlier films, *The Old Plantation* does not feature scenes of masters whipping or auctioning off slaves. An amendment to the Code prevented scenes of brutality, and no cartoon produced after 1934 showed the whipping of slaves or other human characters.

In addition, *The Old Plantation* treats slavery with more reverence than pre-1934 cartoons do. Whereas *Dixie Days* (1930) features slaves skipping and singing on their way to their auctions, *The Old Plantation* illustrates the possibility of the dissolution of a plantation community as a moment of drama. The film promotes slavery as a system of paternalistic white slaveholders caring for grateful, dependent slaves. For example, the slave figures have no relationships among themselves or families of their own. They worry more about losing their master than about suffering the fragmentation of their slave community. The depiction of "massa" as benevolent and fatherly serves to justify the contentment of the slaves under him. Without the theme of paternalism, MGM could not have romanticized slavery as an ideal labor system as blacks and whites competed for work during the depression.[18]

The Old Plantation further stylizes the "peculiar institution" by reducing it to the minstrel songs that lampoon it. The score musically complements the humility of the slave figures and their dependence on the "massa" for survival. In the film's continuity sheet, the character "Black Joe" sings a line from his musical namesake, Stephen Foster's "Old Black Joe," whose lyrics include the words "My head is bending low." The maid character "Aunt Jemima," meanwhile, evokes a song title when declaring the film's plot: "Black Beauty betta win that race or we sho goin' to lose the old Kentucky Home." In addition to these tunes, the film's music score includes bits of Foster's "Camptown Races" and Henry Work's "Jubilo."[19]

In contrast, MGM's *Swing Social* (1940) anachronistically illustrates slave figures by means of jazz music. The film tackles the issue of church truancy, as in *Clean Pastures*, but as more of a musical than as a moral cartoon. As a result, it escaped the attention of the PCA, who had criticized Warner Brothers for its comedic take on truancy. Whereas the truant's punishments for skipping church constitute most of the content of *Clean Pastures*, the focus of *Swing Social is* the enjoyment of black caricatures at a jazzy worship service that a truant is missing. In addition, the characters are black bass named after fictional blacks frequently lampooned by animators, in contrast to the African American comic actors playing biblical characters in *Clean Pastures*. Thus, the actions of fish with names already associated with cartoon comedy—according to the script, "Uncle Tom" and "pickaninnies," for example—attracted less attention than figures named after Saint Peter or the angel Gabriel.[20]

The black characters of *Swing Social* speak in a more racially exaggerated manner than earlier figures had. Even when MGM revamped Bosko as an African American boy, his lines in the scripts for his films did not have nearly as many deliberately misspelled "Negro dialect" words. The script for *Swing Social* demonstrates the problematic writing of dialogue by whites for African Americans. Joseph Barbera, a co-director of the film with William Hanna, stated that his partner had written the script in a stereotypical dialect that black actors whom the studio hired to voice the characters could hardly pronounce. Indeed, Hanna created some complicated words for scat singing in the script. In the twenty-eighth scene, black character Creel Dodger's song about "Good ol' plain fried chicken" includes the unique lyrics, "Skad wadn skoo uh whedd wadn bidd hruppu—pm dee beedle bo."[21]

Meanwhile, cartoon producer Walter Lantz defined his black sharecroppers with different kinds of black music. In *Scrub Me Mama with a Boogie Beat* (1941), nineteenth-century minstrel music accompanies scenes of rural African Americans, while modern boogie-woogie music introduces a shapely urban black female figure. Stephen Foster's "Old Folks at Home" slowly and quietly plays in the background as rural black men doze lazily around Lazytown's cotton bales. Upon the arrival in Lazytown of a young, slender, light-skinned black woman, the music becomes louder, faster, and brassier. The change in tempo signals the sexual arousal of the male characters, who wake from their lethargy to ogle the woman while energetically returning to work. They sing, dance, eat watermelon, and wash clothes to the rhythm of the title song. The dialogue sheet from *Scrub Me Mama with* a *Boogie Beat* identifies the woman as "Nellie (from Harlem)," thus marking one of the first regional differentiations among African Americans in a cartoon. The jazz helps distinguish the northerner from the minstrelsy-defined lazy southerners.

Lantz identified the Lazytowners with pejorative racial slurs, thus marking a new low in African American representation. In one synopsis of *Scrub Me Mama with a Boogie Beat*, the African American male figures—identified as "lazy negro," "coon asleep in fishing boat," and "2 bucks battling"—sit and lie in the fields. In a second synopsis of the cartoon, each African American male character shares the racial slur "nigger" for a name. Some characters are unmotivated to perform even traditional stereotypes: "nigger kids—too tired to eat watermelon." Other characters do not want to expend energy on minute tasks: "nigger smoking pipe—has mule kick him in back—blows smoke ring," and "chickens peck grain off nigger's head to scratch it." One Lazytowner—"nigger fishing—too tired to get off cactus"—simply lacks common sense. Of all the thirteen examples of racial lethargy in the synopsis, only the "niggers—too tired to pick cotton" manage to appear in the film. Whether Lantz or the PCA decided that the other images were too offensive for audiences or too numerous for a six-minute cartoon, the producer had still given the images enough consideration to document them.[22]

Meanwhile, MGM's animators also extracted humor from the poverty and social isolation of African American field laborers, though not as crudely as in Lantz's film. The aforementioned cartoon *The Goose Goes South* (1941) has the unique twist of presenting figures knowledgeable about life outside their cotton plantation. Among the "happy carefree cotton pickers," according to the script, one of the "two negro women in the foreground, picking cotton," complains about her children: "They all wants to grow up to be 'Rochesters.'" The next scene then features "several little pickaninnies" playing with toy telephones, shouting, "Hello, Mr. Benny." Despite the radical image of children looking to a black actor as a role model, the animators tried to extract humor from the juxtaposition of black children looking like poor, exploited rural laborers but acting like a popular contemporary Hollywood performer.[23]

Not every black laborer caricature in cartoons was male. In *Three Orphan Kittens* (1935), Walt Disney resurrected the hefty, desexualized, complaisantly servile "mammy" figure so often found in earlier animated films, but with a twist. In this case the mammy is also religiously devout. She not only sings about her faith while going about her household chores—"Gwine to heaven when I die / Dis sure am a scrumptious pie"—but also demonstrates a sensitivity to moral lessons. What is perhaps most remarkable about this latter trait is that she learns these lessons from a young white girl, presumably the daughter of the servant's employers. In fact, the central plot of the film revolves around the fate of three stray kittens which the mammy proposes to throw out into the snow. When the girl protests, the mammy eventually relents. Left ambiguous is whether the older woman yields because the girl has exerted her moral authority or her social power. But either way, it is clear who holds the position of superiority and who has the attributes of a dependent child.

The devout female servant soon became a standard image of the African American woman in animated as well as live-action films, particularly after Disney's *Three Orphan Kittens* won the Academy Award for Best Cartoon Short Subject of 1935. Earlier stereotypes, such as the scantily clad blues singer featured in Van Beuren's *Magic Art* (1932), disappeared. Whereas the song in that film—"I Ain't Got Nobody"—tells of the woman's troubles in finding a man, lyrics of the PCA era were more likely to focus on the Code-friendly topics of piety and domesticity and avoid altogether the taboo subject of sex. Disney himself capitalized on the success of *Three Orphan Kittens* by producing a sequel, *More Kittens* (1936), starring the same pious black maid.

MGM brought the mammy characterization back to its roots in slavery for the Harman-Ising film *The Old Plantation* (1935). In this film she has her own family and acts as a voice of reason for her slave community. William Hanna and Scott Bradley contributed to the mammy's familial personality through their songwriting talents. They composed the song "Pickin' Cotton," which characters generically named "Aunt Jemima" and "three pickaninnies" sing while performing that chore. According to the film's dialogue cutting continuity, the lyrics are "Pickin' cotton, Mammy's going to show you how / Pickin' cotton, pickaninnies do it now / Pickin' cotton all day long / Pickin' to the rhythm of the cotton pickin' song."[24]

By the end of the 1930s, as animators started using cartoons to poke fun at popular culture, the mammy served as a performer of visual puns in

MGM films. In *The Bookworm* (1939), the mammy figure, yet again named "Aunt Jemima" in the script, contributed to one of animation's few visual puns based on both racial and gender identification. The film consists of a series of book covers coming to life—a popular gimmick originated earlier by Leon Schlesinger's cartoon studio. In one gag from *The Bookworm*, Aunt Jemima emerges from the cover of the novel *Black Beauty*. References to an African American as "black" in the media of the 1930s were not as common as the terms "colored" or "Negro." Nevertheless, the "black" of *Black Beauty* clearly applies to Aunt Jemima's racial identity and "beauty" to her female gender, an often ignored aspect of the mammy characterization, even if intended here as a joke.

The Bookworm illustrates the dominance of white men over black women—content that flirted with violating the Code rule on miscegenation. Parodying both *The Midnight Ride of Paul Revere* and *Black Beauty*, according to the script "Aunt Jemima comes galloping out with Paul Revere riding piggy-back on her." For years American literature by white authors had presented relationships between white men and black women in terms of the woman using her attractiveness and lust to conquer the man; this oversexed female figure served as a rationalization for the rape of female slaves by white masters. Similarly, Paul Revere's riding the mammy symbolizes his sexual conquest of her. In addition, to present the scene effectively, the studio had to make the African American female character behave like a horse. Thus, *The Bookworm* shows the mammy as subhuman as well as racially and sexually inferior. It marked a significant regression; even in Van Beuren's *Dixie Days* (1930), the mammy was able to walk upright on two legs.[25]

In 1940 the studio traded the mammy figure's subhuman sexual characterization for a violent one. Co-directors William Hanna and Joseph Barbera made her a supporting player in "Tom and Jerry" cartoons, in which Tom Cat chases Jerry Mouse. After the United States entered World War II in 1941, Hanna and Barbera fashioned chase scenes after military battles, arming the cat and mouse with weaponry such as grenades, dynamite, and rifles. On occasion Tom and Jerry accidentally attack the maid. The message of the mishaps is that the servant does not belong in the film. She is hurt because she is in the way. For example, Tom mistakes her for a disguised Jerry in the script for *Fraidy Cat* (1942):

Scene 67: Hold scene of the maid's fanny. The cat comes in on her fanny with all four paws and draws up for a big bite.

Scene 68: . . . Off-scene, the maid is heard screaming, "Yipe!" Then she yells sore, "Thomas, you no good cat, attacking from the rear, heh?" . . . The maid continues saying, "Well—take diss you—and diss—."[26]

The script for *The Lonesome Mouse* demonstrates that violence against MGM's maid has misogynistic as well as sexual overtones. Such imagery had actually predated "Tom and Jerry" in animation but had not appeared in cartoons since the establishment of the PCA in 1934. Many of Max Fleischer's "Betty Boop" films contain sexually suggestive images, and cartoon producer Ub Iwerks's film *The Office Boy* (1932) features an extraordinary number of jokes concerning a young woman's posterior. The violence against the mammy character is different, however, because she, unlike Betty, does not have lustful pursuers inflicting violence upon her. In the following scene from *The Lonesome Mouse* (1943), Jerry tortures her:

Scene 39: Cut to the maid sitting on the stove. The little mouse runs up the leg of the stool, jumps up and turns the handle of the gas control. The flame rises in the scene and the maid yells and flies up into the air. The little mouse drops down and runs off scene followed by the cat. Hold the maid off scene and the flame up in the air flickering. (The flame will be like a hand.)

The maid is one of very few animated female characters to receive a deliberate burn on her body. Also, the flame's depiction as a hand implies that the flame fondles her backside, thus adding a sexual dimension to the violent gag.[27]

By severely restricting the mammy's characterization, Hanna and Barbera quickly ran out of new ways to integrate her into the increasingly physical comedy of "Tom and Jerry." In the scripts for the mammy's films, released by MGM between 1940 and 1943, she never appeared in more than 23 percent of a cartoon's scenes. The studio limited her character to either warning Tom not to create a mess at the start of an episode or chastising Tom for doing so at the film's conclusion. The animator Jack Zander, who worked on the early episodes of the series, later attributed the maid's treatment to her weak characterization: "Now the mammy in Tom and Jerry was an outright racist cartoon character. [She] had the typical negro voice and served as a foil for the two animal characters. Showing just her feet and lower body kept us from worrying about her face and making her another "character" to give personality to. A smart move by Joe and Bill, a conscious one, too, I believe."[28]

The co-directors eventually devised new supporting characters to perform the violent scenes. By 1943 Tom had a feline rival in an orange street cat and a canine adversary in Spike the Bulldog, and both characters appeared in several cartoons either to hurt Tom or to receive painful blows from him. After MGM released *The Lonesome Mouse,* the maid did not appear in the series for four years, with the exception of a cameo in *The Mouse Comes to Dinner* (1945). In addition, Hanna-Barbera diversified the settings for the cat and mouse, having them chase each other outside the home in settings ranging from bowling alleys to henhouses. Zander recalled, "As you can see she didn't last long in the series, for the two, Tom and Jerry, became very strong on their own and didn't need any secondary characters to make their story."[29]

MGM's success with the mammy from "Tom and Jerry" proved that this old stock character still had relevance in wartime animation. Its popularity may have had something to do with the increased number of black women in the domestic workforce. As white women left laundry, cafeteria, and maid positions for defense industry employment, African American women had more success finding work in the white women's vacated jobs than in competing with them for defense labor. By 1944, 60 percent of all private domestic employees were black women. As Angela Y. Davis has pointed out, female blues singers frequently sang of the drudgery involved in laundry work; Bessie Smith captured their pain and sorrow in the song "Washwoman Blues."[30]

Like the mammy, the sambo characterization—a gullible and fearful African American boy—received considerable exposure from the Great Depression through World War II. The sambo was the dominant black male animated image of this period, appearing more frequently than adult sharecropper or jazz performer figures. The sambo reflected contemporary Hollywood's exploitation of juvenile actors and characters. Between 1934 and 1938, Shirley Temple was the film industry's top star. Hal Roach's "Our Gang" live-action series starred children, including two African Americans playing the sambo characters Buckwheat and Farina.

Animators soon followed the trend. By 1936 the juvenile Porky Pig had become the star of "Looney Tunes," and Fleischer's "Popeye" cartoons featured sporadic appearances by an infant named Swee'pea. These figures, though white, are juvenile like the sambos; but they were not the only white leading figures in cartoons. In contrast, the immature and weak sambos were the only recurring African American leads in animated films.

The sambo's starring role in his films also distinguishes the characterization from other black animated figures. For example, instead of commenting on the adventures of others as the mammy does, the sambo has his own adventures. Animators had not only the past experience of the silent "Sammy Johnsin" series as a model but also plenty of sambo stories in American literature from which to borrow. The artists could not say the same for the mammy character as a lead.

In 1935 Disney's former right-hand man, Ub Iwerks, produced the first sambo cartoon since "Sammy Johnsin" from his own studio. Titled *Little Black Sambo*, it was loosely based on Helen Bannerman's classic short story for children. Whereas the book tells of Sambo being chased by three tigers that want his clothes, the cartoon shows Sambo pursued by one tiger trying to eat him. In addition to the plot differences, Iwerks adapted Bannerman's characters to suit conventions regarding racial characterization. Bannerman's Sambo has two parents, but the cartoon Sambo's family is typical of Hollywood's standard depiction of black families—a single "mammy" mother and no father. Despite the jungle setting, the mammy speaks as if from the South, calling her son "Honeychild" and telling him to beware of the "bad ol' tiger." As for their visual appearance, the black cartoon characters have the usual liver lips and bug eyes, neither of which appears in the characters in the book.

Iwerks also adapted Sambo and company to the animation trends of the mid-1930s. Sambo looks and acts like Mickey Mouse—hardly a surprise, given that Iwerks helped to create the mouse. The boy is dressed in short pants and huge oval shoes just like Mickey's. In addition, Sambo has an animal sidekick in an unnamed orange dog resembling Mickey's pet orange dog Pluto. The film *Little Black Sambo* was one of several adaptations of children's literature for the "Comicolor" cartoon series Iwerks produced between 1934 and 1936. After the cartoon's theatrical run, it was sold in stores for many years as a film for home projection.

In contrast to Iwerks's Mickey-like Sambo, the Harman-Ising character Bosko was revamped as a sambo in order to make him look *less* like the mouse. Bosko had hardly been the PCA's model character in his "Looney Tunes" episodes. For example, in several episodes he and his co-stars drink alcohol to excess, and his girlfriend Honey dances by suggestively wriggling her hips. At MGM, Harman-Ising cast him in a few unsuccessful cartoons in 1934 and 1935 before dropping him. Then the studio revived Bosko the following year but redesigned him as an African American boy and placed him in a poor, rural environment in order to make him funnier. Mel Shaw recalled that animators tried to extract humor from Bosko by having him perform farming chores. In addition, the studio not only got rid of the references to alcoholism and the hip-wriggling dances but also eliminated Bosko's inconsistency from film to film, which had drawn audiences to his "Looney Tunes" series. In the "Looney Tunes" he plays diverse roles in different settings. In "Happy Harmonies" he is always a boy and always in the South. MGM released episodes of the "Harmonies" Bosko over a period of twenty months—about half the nearly four-year duration of the "Looney Tunes" Bosko series. [31]

By making him more acceptable to the PCA, however, Harman-Ising made Bosko less appealing to audiences. The new format received mixed reviews. One theater manager praised the repetition when reviewing *Bosko and the Cannibals* (1937): "An excellent color cartoon continuing the 'Straight to Grandma's Here I Go' idea that was so effective when Bosko met the Pirates." Another exhibitor, however, considered the familiar storyline of the same film rather boring: "These Bosko cartoons are all the same. Noise and more noise with a caricature of Fats Waller and Cab Calloway, and are getting tiresome. In fact, the song 'Off to Grandma's I Must Go' is getting to be a theme song with them." [32]

Bosko's helplessness and passivity in his final "Happy Harmonies" cartoons in 1937 and 1938, while standard aspects of the sambo characterization, contrast sharply with his "Looney Tunes" persona. As an African American boy, he loses the heroism and confidence that he demonstrated in earlier cartoons when he lacked a clear ethnic identity. With blackness comes cowardice in place of his earlier bravery. When pirates or cannibals chase him in *Bosko and the Pirates* (1937) and *Bosko and the Cannibals* (1937), Bosko can only run away from them. Even Honey, once his damsel in distress, now surpasses him in bravery. While singing of Bosko's fear of ghosts in *The Old House* (1936), she reprimands him: "Bosko I'm ashamed of you / You're a scaredy cat." These films mark a radical departure from earlier "Looney Tunes" films such as *Bosko the Doughboy* (1931), in which he plays a World War I–era soldier, and *Beau Bosko* (1933), in which he is a Legionnaire battling a powerful desert villain.[33]

For Bosko's last three cartoons, Harman-Ising returned to its winning formula from the "Looney Tunes" series—exploiting contemporary music. Each episode is a musical in which the boy imagines encountering the jazz frogs while delivering cookies to his grandmother. However, reflecting the new Code era, the songs are not about alcohol or sex but rather about the cookies; the studio's composers wrote original songs about the desire of the frogs to eat the snacks. Moreover, the caricatures of Louis Armstrong, Fats Waller, Cab Calloway, and others do all the singing and dancing, thus rendering Bosko a supporting figure in his own episodes despite all the changes Harman-Ising made to him. The studio no longer trusted its longtime star to carry his films by himself. An advertisement for *Bosko and the Cannibals* in the newspaper *Atlanta Constitution* even promoted the film as "*Bosko and the Cannibals* with Cab Calloway, Louis Armstrong and Others."[34]

Walter Lantz's "Li'l Eightball" series simultaneously adheres to and lampoons traditional racial generalizations. In the tradition of stump speeches performed by blackface minstrels, the young Eightball occasionally recites lengthy monologues in "Negro dialect" featuring polysyllabic words. When confronted by ghosts who tried to scare him in *A-Haunting We Will Go* (1939), he remarks, "In this enlightened age, we childrens do not recognize ectoplasmic figments of the imagination." He later declares, "This exhibition of supernatural claptrap don't affect me in the least." Lantz used Eightball's fearlessness as a source of ironic humor for audiences expecting a frightened boy. The producer also, however, made him fearful in order to bring the cartoon to a credible resolution. By running away from the ghosts at the end of the cartoon, he demonstrates African Americans' presumed helplessness and passivity. The cowardly image, thus counterbalances Eightball's radically brave characterization.[35]

Through this sambo figure, Lantz pushed the Hays Code to its limits. The "Eightball" cartoons poked fun at the "moral cartoon" trend created in response to the PCA. In the films Li'l Eightball does not learn valuable life lessons but learns rather to conform to ethnic stereotypes in changing from an atypically self-assured and brave African American boy character to a paranoid and fearful one. He begins each cartoon by denying the existence of the curses and ghosts that he comes to acknowledge at the film's end. In *Silly Superstition* (1939), he tells his dog that superstitions are not real, but he himself becomes a believer after his encounter with a lion. Like his white juvenile "moral cartoon" counterparts, however, Li'l Eightball is tormented by predators such as lions and ghosts before learning his "lesson" in African American behavior. The moral ambiguity of the "Eightball" cartoons and the lack of originality in characterization earned mixed reviews from exhibitors and a short life for the series, which died after only three episodes. A. J. Inks of the *Motion Picture Herald* called *Silly Superstition* "just a fair cartoon" and reported that *A-Haunting We Will Go* earned "no laughs."[36]

So pervasive in American culture was the sambo by the early 1940s that foreign animators sought to capitalize on its popularity. For Paramount Pictures Corporation, George Pal, a Hungarian immigrant, created the animated sambo figure "Jasper," who gullibly falls for the schemes of a scarecrow and a crow. Pal claimed that his fondness for American folklore naturally led him to adapt the sambo characterization to animation. To be sure, Jasper's episodes are on a par with contemporary sambo films from other producers such as Ub Iwerks and Harman-Ising, for their films have rural settings and characters who speak "in dialect." The character's only unique trait lay in how Pal animated him: he used the process of pixillation—filming puppets in different poses and lip positions to simulate the movement and speech of characters, as opposed to drawing them on celluloid sheets.[37]

The "Jasper" films were popular with theater critics, audiences, and AMPAS. Pal featured the character in cartoons from 1942 to 1947—the longest run of all the sambo figures. In addition, Jasper is the only animated sambo to star in a film nominated for an Academy Award. Part of the fascination for viewers of the character related to the novelty of pixillation; when *Time* magazine covered Jasper's debut in *Jasper and the Watermelons* (1942), the periodical gave more attention to the film process than to the plot or the characterizations. Pal also incorporated lots of familiar racial comedy in his films, which usually drew laughs. For example, the shot *Time* used from the cartoon featured Jasper lusting over watermelon. Films also contain jokes about life during World War II such as a reference to the military draft in *Jasper and the Haunted House* (1942).[38]

Other studios followed Pal's lead in modernizing the sambo figure. For example, the sambo characters from the new Schlesinger Productions director Chuck Jones perform violent slapstick wartime humor, despite their roots in earlier studio cartoons. His "Merrie Melodie" cartoon *Flop Goes the Weasel* (1943) stars a black-feathered bird who, while still inside his egg, accidentally rolls away from his kerchief-wearing mammy and mistakes a predatory weasel for his mother upon hatching. Although the little bird's loquaciousness is borrowed from Jones's little mouse character Sniffles, the bird speaks in stereotypical African American speech. His violent tormenting of the weasel while innocently calling her "Mammy" originates with Schlesinger's "Merrie Melodies" episode *A Tale of Two Kitties* (1942), in which Tweety physically injures two predatory cats while lamenting in a baby-talk voice, "Poor little puddy-tats." Despite the similarities to other studio figures, the blackbird exhibits obvious African American stereotypes. Exhibitor Besa Short identified some of them in her description of the film: "Latest Merrie Melody brings a loquacious little chicken and his coal black mammy. In a deep South locale, Mammy is a knittin' and a sittin' when all of a sudden, bang—out cracks junior all black and with a full blown Southern accent."[39]

Jones proved in *Flop Goes the Weasel* that traditional African American characterizations could be adapted to experimental stylized settings and physical humor. He used flat-colored backgrounds for this film, a technique he had originated with his cartoon *The Dover Boys* (1942). As cartoon studios were still producing highly detailed settings for their characters, Jones's cartoon marked a radical artistic departure. In addition, the film's protagonist displays sadism that contrasts with the introspectiveness of earlier films' characters. These figures—Sniffles and an African pygmy caricature named Inki, who appeared in five films between 1939 and 1950—wrung more humor from facial expressions than from action. *Flop Goes the Weasel*, however, contains strong slapstick gags, such as the bird burning the weasel's foot and hitting him on the head with a mallet.

The humor in Jones's "Looney Tune" episode *Angel Puss* (1944) depends even more heavily on racial stereotypes than *Flop Goes the Weasel*. In the film an African American boy, whom Jones's script identifies as "Sambo," feels guilty about drowning a cat for money. The cat, having escaped the drowning, then torments Sambo by dressing as a ghost and scaring him. As a caricature of Stepin' Fetchit, Sambo has a lethargic manner and sleepy eyes. The caricature itself is not visually original; a sambo character in the "Merrie Melodies" film *All This and Rabbit Stew* (1941) exhibits the same demeanor and even wears the same clothing—a hat, short-sleeved shirt, overalls, and oversized shoes. Sambo also speaks in malapropisms, as had the Fetchit caricatures of the mid-1930s. In Jones's dialogue sheet for the cartoon, many jokes are based on Sambo's stereotypical speech, as opposed to the physical gags in *Flop Goes the Weasel*. When looking at a river before tossing a cat into it, Sambo declares, "Dat is da most discomfortable lookin' water us ever did see," then redundantly exclaims, "Dat sho' is wet watah!" Other Fetchit-inspired gags focus on the boy's superstitious fear of ghosts. When the cat then disguises himself as the ghost of his supposedly drowned self, the boy reacts to his presence with a series of wide-eyed expressions of fright. Making a reference to a black comedian's tagline "Feet, don't fail me now," Jones's script calls for Sambo to shout, "Git goin', feet," when approached by the "ghost."[40]

Jones advanced his methods of visual humor and comic timing in *Angel Puss*. He drew humor from facial expressions by creating comic "takes"—looks of surprise or fright—for Sambo. The film's graveyard scenes provide a perfect setting for Sambo to express fear. Whenever he sees or hears the ghost cat, his sleepy eyes bug out of their sockets or pop out beneath his oversized hat. Jones stylized the animation as well. Sambo often appears as a blur or a smear when fleeing the ghost, accentuating how swiftly he runs from it. Such smearing and then popping into a normal design when a character stops running characterized the body of Jones's later work as a director. His cartoons starring the Road Runner (1949–64) show the bird smearing and popping during chase scenes, while hapless predator Wile E. Coyote expresses stylized looks of pain or frustration at assorted explosions and accidents resulting from falling boulders.

Sambo in *Angel Puss* is as violent as the bird of *Flop Goes the Weasel*. In *Angel Puss* the black figure does not become aggressive until he discovers the cat's disguise. Sambo then fires his rifle and kills the cat. This intentional act of violence performed out of rage is thus contextually different from the brutal scenes of the bird "accidentally" hurting the cat in *Flop Goes the Weasel.*

By keeping Sambo and other black characterizations consistent while changing story formulas, most cartoon studios survived the depression and World War II. Meanwhile, during this same period, Schlesinger director Fred "Tex" Avery advanced the animated cartoon by using African American cultural expression instead of showing black figures fostered by whites. He constructed jokes and characters with a black aesthetic, creating a new star in the process—Bugs Bunny.

FOUR

Fred "Tex" Avery and
"Trickster" Animation

Frederick Bean "Tex" Avery, who directed cartoons for Leon Schlesinger Productions from 1935 to 1941, often gave them a very unlikely African American aesthetic. No scholarship on animation reveals the remotest familiarity on Avery's part with black culture. A white man from Texas, he frequently resorted to ethnic stereotypes—especially African American ones—for humor in his films. When he decided to develop unique ways of getting laughs from film audiences, however, he drew on elements of African American expression that had been integrated into American culture for generations.

Avery set himself apart from other directors by pioneering "trickster animation." While his contemporaries continued to make animated musicals and melodramas, he deliberately sought to fool audiences with cinematic pranks. For example, stories often had titles that were obvious puns such as Friz Freleng's *Clean Pastures*, playing on *The Green Pastures;* the phrases sounded similar, and both were connected to films about blacks. In contrast, one of Avery's early cartoons, *Golddiggers of '49* (1936), displays a glitzy title card suggesting the famous troupe of showgirls. The film is not about chorus girls, however, but about Western prospectors searching for gold. Avery, in signifying one genre of Hollywood film (the lavish musical) to represent another (the Western), employed a common device in the folktales of black slaves—deception as a means of humor. Such stories are often moral tales concerning a "trickster" character who acts in a certain manner in order to manipulate the behavior of another figure, especially an adversary. Avery made audiences think that they were about to see one kind of film then fooled them with a completely different kind of picture by capitalizing on the duplicitous cultural meaning of "golddigger."

Avery also drew humor from visual duplicity in the film *Uncle Tom's*

Bungalow (1937), which pokes fun at the "plantation melodrama" film genre of the 1930s. The cartoon looks like previous takeoffs on Harriet Beecher Stowe's famous novel, featuring plenty of scenes of cotton fields and wooden shacks. As usual, Uncle Tom appears as an old man, shaking violently as he walks down a dirt road in his first scene. Avery counts on viewers to equate the slave figure's jerkiness with his age. When the off-screen narrator addresses Tom's instability, however, the old man replies, "Brudah, 'ma' knees ain't shakin. Ah's truckin'! La-de-ah!" The joke itself is duplicitous in nature, for Avery not only manages to trick the audience by making Tom's dancing look like an elderly man's walk but also throws in anachronistic humor by having the slave speak in modern slang.[1]

After *Uncle Tom's Bungalow*, Avery kept experimenting with trickster animation. He deceived audiences first by making realistically designed characters behave in a surprising manner. For example, in his parodies of travelogue documentaries, animal figures moving very much like their live-action counterparts calmly and unexpectedly respond in wisecracks to off-screen narrators. In *Wacky Wildlife* (1940), a camel wandering in a desert stops the narrator's bragging about the animal's remarkable hydration to counter quietly but emphatically, "I don't care what you say. I'm thirsty." Such gags originate from folktale trickery as well as nineteenth-century minstrel shows, in which "endmen" characters shouted barbs and danced around the stage—all to the dismay of the dignified, reserved master of ceremonies or "interlocutor."

In addition, the relaxed demeanor of the camel coincides with an emerging African American cultural style, perhaps best epitomized by the groundbreaking bebop musician Lester Young. In the 1940s Young disregarded the showmanship and flamboyant gestures of his more famous contemporaries, such as the dancing of Cab Calloway and Louis Armstrong's dabbing of his forehead with his handkerchief. To him such actions were superficial, clownish distractions from performing music. Instead, he maintained a reserved bearing both on and off stage and distanced himself from audiences by wearing sunglasses while performing. His audiences, initially taken aback, eventually embraced his "cool" pose.[2]

Within a year of developing this African American cultural approach to cartoon humor, Avery developed a star for it. His previous films focused more on gags than on characterization. For each phony travelogue, he used between seven and ten short gags and cast a different character in each scene. As a result, no particular character stands out from another. Meanwhile, he also used visual duplicity for films starring established characters such as Porky Pig. In *Porky's Duck Hunt* (1937), a realistic-looking mallard swims about until the pig shoots at him. The duck then suddenly becomes anthropomorphic, crossing his eyes, talking with a lisp, hyperactively jumping and hooting at random intervals, and pulling objects out of thin air. The duck—later named Daffy—was an entertaining change from the mild-mannered animal stars of Walt Disney's films, and *Porky's Duck Hunt* became an immediate hit.

The studio subsequently made additional films in which animals frustrate hunters with their lunacy. Fellow director Ben "Bugs" Hardaway borrowed from Avery to develop a cross-eyed bunny with a frenetic chuckle and an aggressive streak. The rabbit, however, did not instantly win over audiences. He was more aggressive than Daffy, often deliberately antagonizing hunters instead of acting in self-defense. Still, Schlesinger allowed Hardaway and other directors to make more cartoons starring the bunny.

Then, in the summer of 1940, the character finally developed into an even more popular muse than Daffy. Avery's "Merrie Melodies" cartoon *A Wild Hare* (1940) opens with recurring star Elmer Fudd hunting rabbits. As he searches one hole, a rabbit pops out of an adjacent one, bravely steps toward Elmer and his gun, and calmly asks, "What's up, Doc?" The director later recalled that the audience watching the film with him was taken by surprise not only by the line but also by the character's nonchalant delivery of it. At that moment the rabbit broke away from his wild, unstable contemporaries. To be sure, the rabbit is somewhat similar to Hardaway's in that both pull pranks on hunters. Avery's rabbit, however, neither antagonizes Elmer nor laughs in spite of himself. In addition, while Hardaway's bunny's tended to pull props out of thin air, Avery's rabbit uses only his wits to defeat the hunter. The film is a clever twist on the "hunter versus animal" formula that Avery himself had created in *Porky's Duck Hunt*.

More important, Avery made the rabbit unique by combining figures from African American slave folktales with the bebop aesthetic. According to Ralph Ellison in *Shadow and Act*, bebop music created excitement in its listeners, though the musicians themselves did not become excitable. Another important element of bebop was aloofness in the face of violence or evil. Accordingly, the rabbit never expresses any fear of losing his life to Elmer's gun. As for the folkloric aspect of the characterization, the animation historian Joe Adamson traces the rabbit's roots specifically to Joel Chandler Harris's character Br'er Rabbit, showing that Harris's book *Uncle Remus: His Songs and Sayings*, which appropriated stories from African American slaves, in turn supplied some of the gags for the films. Indeed, both characters share the traits of confidence and cleverness, and both are willing to feign humility in the process of outsmarting their adversaries.[3]

The rabbit demonstrates his black cultural characterization throughout *A Wild Hare*. For example, near the end of the cartoon, he allows hunter Elmer Fudd to shoot him. This action exemplifies bebop, because the rabbit remains calm and sociable amidst violence. He knows that Fudd is a poor marksman; after all, at the beginning of the film Fudd converses with him before recognizing him as the prey. The rabbit's generosity also illustrates his folktale roots, because he allows the hunter to think that he has been successful in the hunt. Br'er Rabbit does the same thing in *Uncle Remus*, convincingly pleading with his captor not to throw him into the briar patch he calls "home." In another echo of folklore, the rabbit further fabricates vulnerability by faking his own death after Elmer fires the gun. This gag recalls three *Uncle Remus* stories: "Mr. Wolf Makes a Failure," "Mr. Fox Tackles Old Man Tarrypin," and "Mr. Fox Goes A-Hunting, but Mr. Rabbit Bags the Game" all feature anthropomorphic animals who pretend to be dead.[4]

The line "What's up, Doc" perfectly encapsulates Avery's African American aesthetic all by itself. By posing the question, the rabbit again exemplifies the folktale character's false vulnerability by pretending not to know the hunter's intentions. At the same time, his unflappable demeanor in the face of an obvious threat is the very embodiment of the bebop idea of "cool." As Joel Dinerstein has argued, in its origins the West African notion of "coolness" was associated with good-humored people unwilling to let hardships faze them; they were neither icy social loners nor happy "darkies" using smiles and shuffles as masks. In his confrontation with Elmer Fudd, the rabbit displays the same affect. Instead of challenging the hunter or fleeing in fright, he calmly asks, "What's up, Doc," inviting dialogue and disarming his opponent by defying expectations. There is also an element of coded language in his pet phrase of the sort sometimes used by blacks when confronted with racism. For him to say "You don't scare me" would have created instant tension between himself and the hunter. "What's up, Doc" demonstrates the same bravado under the guise of friendliness and innocent curiosity.[5]

The character immediately created a sensation with viewers and in the film industry. *A Wild Hare* won an Academy Award nomination for best cartoon short subject, and exhibitors called for more cartoons starring the understated rabbit. Schlesinger christened him "Bugs Bunny," since he considered Avery's rabbit to have originated as Bugs Hardaway's bunny, although most Schlesinger employees saw the rabbit and the bunny as two entirely different characters. Meanwhile, Hollywood studios tried to duplicate the Schlesinger's success with Bugs by creating clever animal figures, but they were pale imitations of the original. Characters such as the Crow from Columbia Pictures' "The Fox and the Crow" series fail to exhibit the cool that made Bugs different from both Disney's passive stars and Schlesinger's wacky characters.[6]

Bugs Bunny's stardom also affected cartoon production in New York. In 1942 Paramount Pictures fired the Fleischer brothers from their own studio and promoted animators Seymour Kneitel and Isadore Sparber to co-producers. The following year the recently established Famous Studios launched the "Noveltoons" series as a testing ground for new characters. At first these films featured hip tricksters such as Blackie the Lamb and Buzzy the Crow, but these figures did not achieve anything like the success of Bugs Bunny. The series later hit its stride with cute characters such as Casper the Friendly Ghost (1948–59) and the precocious moppet Little Audrey (1948–58). Famous relied on trickster imagery one last time in the 1950s with episodes based on the theme "Mr. Rabbit Finds His Match at Last." These derivative films starred the characters Tommy Tortoise and Moe Hare.

Also in New York, the Terrytoons studio, now producing for Twentieth Century–Fox, developed its own clones of the rabbit by splitting the be-bop-folktale aesthetic between individual figures. In 1945 the artists took the novel approach of creating an identical pair of talking magpies. Terrytoons christened the twosome "Heckle" and "Jeckle." The bird with the British accent exhibited the refined, humble aspects of the folktale figure. His accomplice, speaking as if from the urban northern United States, displayed bebop's cool. For over two decades, they starred in dozens of episodes, working in tandem to frustrate and defeat their opponents. They signaled Paul Terry's acknowledgment of the popularity of the bunny and his embrace of contemporary characterizations. Before 1945 his stars were the daydreaming Gandy Goose, whose episodes owe a debt to the "Sammy Johnsin" series, and the diminutive but formidable rodent Mighty Mouse, a parody of Max Fleischer's defunct "Superman" cartoon series.

Ironically, Avery himself did not initially appreciate Bugs's audience appeal. Instead of capitalizing on the popularity of his emerging star, he developed new cartoon characters with similar traits. In *The Crackpot Quail* (1941), the title star, like the rabbit, nonchalantly faces danger; the quail playfully goads a hunting dog and even calls his hunter "Doc." Unlike the rabbit, however, the bird barely interacts with the dog. In addition, *The Crackpot Quail* lacks a strong conclusion that would show the quail as victorious over the dog. The bird merely manages to make the clumsy dog crash into trees; nor does the dog sulk away in defeat. Despite the similarities, the quail failed to catch on with audiences. Avery wisely returned to the rabbit, making three more episodes before leaving Schlesinger's studio in 1941.

The episode *Tortoise Beats Hare* (1941) uses the bebop-folktale imagery but from a different angle. The cartoon retells the *Uncle Remus* story "Mr. Rabbit Finds His Match at Last," in which a turtle cheats in a running race with a rabbit by scattering lookalike turtles throughout the course. In this film the rabbit becomes the tricked instead of the trickster, demonstrating his folktale roots by showing overconfidence in claiming an easy victory over the tortoise. The tortoise, meanwhile, exhibits bebop-like calm by grinning while silently accepting Bugs's threats and taunts.[7]

Avery's next two films starring the rabbit reveal the weakness of the director's weaving of bebop and folktales into the character's personality. The rabbit's bebop-derived bravery in confronting a hunter provided the humor in the introductory scenes. Then the jokes borrowed from folktales make for strong gags that entertained audiences through the middle scenes. But because Avery's cartoons substituted strings of gags for stories with firm plots, he needed to finish his films with a strong conclusion, as in *A Wild Hare*. In these two episodes, he failed to do so.

In *All This and Rabbit Stew* (1941), Avery almost returned Bugs to the bebop-folktale fusion he had perfected in *A Wild Hare*. He draws from slaves' stories by having the bunny outsmart an African American hunter and engage in casual dialogue with the character. And the director elaborates on the first film's bebop scene of Bugs' encounter with the hunter by having the rabbit lie on the hunter's gun while posing his famous catchphrase. But Avery deviates sharply from what he had established as his star's unique personality by showing him in a genuine panic: in one scene Bugs screams when he sees the hunter instantly reappear behind him after having fallen off a cliff mere seconds earlier. In addition, the film's conclusion, in which Bugs challenges the African American to a game of craps, is uncharacteristic of his personality. When Bugs produces dice out of thin air, he recalls Hardaway's bunny. Furthermore, in challenging the hunter to gamble, Bugs relies on luck instead of his wits. Finally, the gambling gag is an unnecessary kowtowing by Avery to ethnic stereotyping.

Although *The Heckling Hare* (1941) contains no jokes made at the expense of African Americans, it too presents Bugs in an uncharacteristic manner. To be sure, in several scenes he acts like his old, black cultural self. He playfully engages with a hunting dog in ways that recall his initial bebop indifference to Elmer Fudd's gun. In another example of coded behavior, he insults the dog by kissing him—a tactic borrowed from silent actor Charlie Chaplin—instead of bragging, "I've just tricked you." He draws from folktales by faking his death, but once again he loses his "cool" in the end by screaming as he and the dog fall endlessly from the sky.[8]

For all the ambiguities embodied in Bugs Bunny's character, the films in which he starred made Warner Brothers a formidable force in the animation industry. Most historians of American animation agree that during World War II, Walt Disney's cartoon shorts lost their dominance with audiences. Scholars differ, however, as to why these changes took place. Leonard Maltin notes that by the 1940s, Disney had settled into story formulas for his characters and prioritized personality animation over strong action sequences. Indeed, during World War II, Donald Duck often played a clumsy soldier, and several "Goofy" episodes contain significant lulls in the action for the dog to smile at viewers or scratch his head in confusion. The animator and author Shamus Culhane, however, is also correct in judging that the brashness of the Warner Brothers cartoons provided a fresh approach to cartoon humor, which Disney and other studios soon adopted. For example, Disney appropriated Avery's travelogue parodies for the "Goofy" series during the 1940s and 1950s. In many of the films the dog countermands all the steps in an off-screen narrator's instructions on how to do something by ineptly performing each act.[9]

Still, after *A Wild Hare* even the animated travelogues became passé, and Disney failed to create an aesthetic of humor to challenge Avery's successfully. The studio never grasped Avery's application of folktales and be-bop to animation. Instead of drawing from African American creativity, Disney borrowed from nineteenth-century blackface minstrelsy. As for the wartime films in which Donald Duck plays the role of a conscripted army private, gags involving his ineptitude at following orders and his clumsiness with weapons had first appeared in minstrel shows lampooning African American soldiers of the Civil War. Meanwhile, in the new "Goofy" cartoons, the star plays the "endman," while the narrator serves as the "interlocutor." The dog trips and falls across the screen when clumsily trying to follow the narrator's directions, thus resembling the loud, unhinged minstrel characters instead of the dignified camel of *Wacky Wildlife.*[10]

Meanwhile, Avery jeopardized his own tenure at Schlesinger Productions by behaving like a bebop artist himself. Such performers avoided the exploitation of their music—for example, crass commercialization by movie studios and other enterprises concerned mostly with maximizing profits. Avery likewise winced at producer Schlesinger's efforts to soften Bugs's image as a means of marketing the character. The director hated the name "Bugs Bunny"; he had created a rabbit, not a cute bunny. When interviewed in the 1960s and 1970s, he still referred to Bugs as a rabbit. Avery left the studio in 1941, after Schlesinger had censored *The Heckling Hare*'s original ending, in which Bugs and the dog fell to their deaths. Avery never made another "Bugs Bunny" episode.[11]

Directors of "Bugs Bunny" films after 1941 brought the character to unprecedented heights for a cartoon figure but destroyed the African American identity of Avery's rabbit in the process. They failed to grasp the black aesthetic that Avery had perfected. Bugs no longer exhibited a "cool" but humble demeanor. He became cockier and spent less time pretending to play a timid and defenseless animal for predators. Bugs's personality reverted to that of Hardaway's bunny, as directors made him more hyperactive and more physically violent toward his adversaries. Whereas audience response to Hardaway's figure had been lukewarm, however, viewers embraced the more abrasive Bugs. In 1944 the "Bugs Bunny" series replaced Disney's cartoons as the most popular short subjects among exhibitors annually polled by the trade journal *Motion Picture Herald*.[12]

Bugs's rising popularity after Avery's departure had at least as much to do with changes in American culture and society as with any modifications of his design and character. Avery's sedate, cordial, and unflappable character had more relevance for audiences in 1940 than in 1941. The difference was America's entrance into World War II after Japan's attack on Pearl Harbor. As the United States joined the Allies to fight the Axis, domestic movies and radio programs promoted the characterization of the tough, abrasive American soldier. Likewise, Schlesinger's directors transformed Bugs into more of an aggressive fighter and less a playful woodland creature. Making the wartime symbolism less subtle, Freleng pitted Bugs against caricatures of Adolf Hitler and Hermann Goering in *Herr Meets Hare* (1944) and against Japanese soldier figures in *Bugs Bunny Nips the Nips* (1944).

Chuck Jones, who took over from Avery and directed Bugs Bunny for the next twenty-two years, never embraced the character's African American aesthetic. In contrast to the friendliness and self-confidence that had characterized Avery's rabbit, Jones made Bugs at once insecure and harder edged. For example, in *Elmer's Pet Rabbit* (1941), in which Elmer Fudd takes Bugs home to keep him as a pet, Jones borrows his predecessor's "phony death" gag by having Bugs pretend to drown. Unlike in Avery's films, however, Jones—formerly an animator for Avery—removes the element of surprise from the scene by having Bugs announce his intention to fake his death. Instead of boldly embracing a confrontation initiated by Elmer, the less self-assured Bugs causes conflict in order to control his situation. Displaying extreme rudeness, the bunny leaves his outdoor cage and invades Elmer's home, imposing upon him. These actions, as well as Bugs's perpetual scowl in the film, are completely without the bebop-derived quality of cordiality toward adversaries. In addition, lacking folktale humility, the bunny slaps Elmer in the face with a glove. In later episodes the bunny more subtly expresses contempt for his foes, sometimes simply raising an eyebrow or yawning in their presence.

Jones's studio colleague Friz Freleng also made additions to Bugs Bunny's persona while disregarding Avery's original concept. *Hiawatha's Rabbit Hunt* (1941) offers even less of the bebop-folktale combination than *Elmer's Pet Rabbit*. At no point in the cartoon does Bugs feign weakness or humility. Replicating the iciness of Jones's version of Bugs, Freleng's bunny does not playfully interact with Hiawatha but seeks to escape the hunter and humiliate him. In so doing, he becomes an edgier figure than Avery's rabbit. The bunny ties the "native" to a totem pole and taunts him with a dance. Freleng also introduces the bunny's use of costume disguises, thus bringing an element of vaudeville to the series. Resorting to ethnic stereotyping, the director dresses Bugs as a Native American—an appearance that fools his Indian predator. More important, Freleng violates a central, if unspoken, rule of folktales that the trickster has to be smaller or weaker than his opponent; Bugs towers over the diminutive Hiawatha. Freleng often designed the bunny's adversaries as small but aggressive figures who fail to catch him because of their own shortcomings, such as the impatience of the cowboy character Yosemite Sam.

Warner director Bob Clampett's swing aesthetic contrasted dramatically with Avery's bebop aesthetic and Freleng's aggressive conception of the bunny. Clampett's characters generally stretch their body parts to exaggerated proportions, scream their dialogue, and move quickly. Clampett—another of Avery's former animators—often presented these actions by referring to African American culture, for example, having animals dance the jitterbug or shout "jive" slang. The swing aesthetic did not work for all of his cartoons, however. It was a good fit for the urban African American characters of his film *Coal Black an de Sebben Dwarfs* (1942) but clashed with Avery's "cool" bunny. Clampett's exaggerated directing style resulted in more antagonistic behavior from Bugs than in Avery's episodes. This aggressive depiction of the character is ironic, because both directors borrowed from *Uncle Remus* for their respective interpretations of the bunny. In Clampett's *Wabbit Twouble* (1941), Bugs plays tricks on Elmer Fudd without provocation. Fudd is a vacationer in a park, not a hunter, and he provides no physical threat to Bugs. The bunny therefore behaves like the "Br'er Rabbit" character in stories such as "Miss Cow Falls a Victim to Mr. Rabbit," in which the rabbit tricks an unsuspecting and vulnerable cow. Bugs's cruelty and lack of humility toward Fudd make him an unsympathetic and, consequently, unappealing character.[13]

The last break from Avery's version of Bugs was visual. In 1943 animator Robert McKimson redesigned the bunny for a model sheet—a series of poses and facial expressions for a character used by all the artists working on a film to maintain consistency in the figure's appearance. McKimson made Bugs's face circular instead of oval. The artist also rounded the bunny's eyes and gave the cheeks a more pronounced appearance. Bugs was transformed into something Avery had specifically avoided: a "cute" character.

As for Avery, he relocated to Metro-Goldwyn-Mayer's cartoon department, where he stayed for over a decade. He continued to integrate aspects of bebop into his films. His gags became stronger, and his comic timing improved. He developed an animation style that enhanced humor by requiring fewer drawings than "realistic" animation—yet another break from the industry's status quo. The sketches produced by his animators emphasized the timing of the figures' movements. Thus, Avery derived humor not only from what characters did but also from how they moved while performing the actions. He had a larger budget than at Warner Brothers, which allowed him to experiment in extracting humor from Technicolor and other technological processes while continuing to create unexpected "trickster" cartoon gags for realistically animated characters. Most historians concur that his years at MGM represented his creative peak.[14]

His tenure at MGM, however, did not yield any major stars. The distributor hoped that the director could create a star character for them, just as he had made Bugs Bunny for Warner Brothers. He does not seem to have tried terribly hard to satisfy his new employer's wish. The majority of his films were gag compilations without stars. He had respectable success with the laconic and reserved Droopy Dog, but characters such as Screwy Squirrel and the bears George and Junior (poking fun at John Steinbeck's novel *Of Mice and Men*) did not last beyond five films each.

Among Avery's MGM stars, Screwy is most similar to Bugs. The squirrel draws significantly from the characters of slave folktales. He enjoys being chased and thrives on manipulating adversaries with his false humility. He differs from Bugs only by insensitively pointing and laughing at his pursuers when they falter. Nevertheless, this deviation from Bugs makes Screwy even more similar to Br'er Rabbit, who teases Br'er Fox for trapping him but then inadvertently returning him to his briar patch.

In contrast to Screwy, the diminutive Droopy lacks the intellectual and emotional dimensions of Bugs Bunny's African American characteristics. To be sure, he, like Bugs, is unfazed when confronted by much taller antagonists. He does not outwit them, however, but rather surprises them by unexpectedly sneaking up behind them once they think they have killed him. He occasionally resorts to violence, beating them with his fists despite his small size, a toughness that also deviates from the humility of folktale animals and their exclusive exercise of mental rather than physical skills. In addition, he maintains a deadpan expression and displays no joy in teasing his opponents. In this respect he more closely resembles the cold, icy loner of Western literature, not the jovial African "cool" figure. His adversaries, usually a wolf or a bulldog, elicit almost all the laughs of the series; they react with bugged eyes and dropped jaws whenever encountering the dog after having tried to kill him. Droopy's minimal contributions consist of brief lines such as "Guess who," "That makes me mad," and "You know what? I'm happy."[15]

With Bugs's post-Avery personality changes and the director's creation of the "uncool" Droopy, a brief moment in African American representation in animation had passed. In his short tenure at Leon Schlesinger Productions, Avery proved that directors could borrow from African American culture without exploiting or stereotyping black people. The convergence of old and new African American tropes, as manifested in his version of Bugs Bunny, disappeared within a year of his being fired by Schlesinger. Only Bugs had the bebop "cool" to complement his folk-derived cunning, and only Avery succeeded in integrating the two. Yet the practice of manipulating black culture for artistic and other reasons continued. The next chapter discusses the deliberate compromising of controversial black political expressions by white animators during World War II.

FIVE

Black Representation and World War II Political Concerns

From the very beginning of America's involvement in World War II, the blackface image contributed to the war effort of the U.S. animation industry. Leon Schlesinger Productions started work on the war bonds commercial *Leon Schlesinger Presents Bugs Bunny* in late November 1941, completing it only eight days after Japan attacked Pearl Harbor on December 7. According to the *Hollywood Reporter*, a cartoon of similar length and quality usually took two months to produce. The film displays patriotic symbols such as Bugs dressed as Uncle Sam, and he, Porky Pig, and Elmer Fudd wear American army uniforms while singing the song "Any Bonds Today." The cartoon places blackface minstrelsy within the context of these national symbols. Bugs puts on blackface makeup and imitates Al Jolson, singing "Sammy," a reference to Uncle Sam as well as to Jolson's popular theme song, "Mammy." Bugs's appearance in blackface correlated with the trend at the time for white characters to wear blackface in live-action movie musicals; this genre of film celebrated blackface minstrelsy as the only form of popular entertainment to have originated in America. Thus blackface, with its uniquely American roots, was considered a patriotic image.[1]

African American stereotypes had become so ingrained in American animation by World War II that gags such as Bugs Bunny's Jolson imitation seemed only natural to white animators. The blackface character, though no longer a dominant image in animated cartoons, was still familiar to audiences, and studios tended to use it in brief scenes to add humorous touches to musical cartoons, thus, relying on blackface even when it was not central to a cartoon. As Martha Sigall, who painted celluloid sheets for the film, remembered: "I don't think that *Any Bonds Today* needed the black face segment. But I also don't feel that it hindered it, either." She recalled that the scene accounted for only ten of the ninety seconds of the film's duration. Indeed, the parody did not add to or detract from the film's central message, "Buy war bonds." But neither did blackface help endear the cartoon to black viewers.[2]

In fact, the appearance of century-old racial caricature in wartime cartoons like *Leon Schlesinger Presents Bugs Bunny* did not sit well with a number of Americans. Ever since the first release of the pro–Ku Klux Klan movie *Birth of a Nation* (1916), individuals and organizations devoted to the cause of civil rights had lodged complaints with Hollywood studios about the derogatory treatment of African Americans in motion pictures. They called on the studios to develop roles beyond servant characters for African American actors and to end "sambo" and "mammy" depictions altogether. Hollywood initially paid little attention to the concerns of the activists. As outsiders to the film industry, they lacked the power to influence either the business practices of studio executives or the creative decisions of writers and directors. Their arguments hit home during World War II, however, by effectively associating the filmed stereotypes with racism in the United States and around the world.

The struggle against the fascist Axis powers raised questions about the social status and civil rights of African Americans that had been too long ignored. In 1942, in the African American newspaper the *Pittsburgh Courier*, reporter William Nunn coined the phrase "Double V," which meant victory both abroad in World War II and at home against Jim Crow. Some African Americans who fought in or supported the war hoped that their liberation of Europe from Hitler's "master race" plan would result in the dismantling of Jim Crow laws in the United States. Under the banner of the newspaper's "Double V" campaign, the journalists frequently cited incidents of domestic violence against African Americans and reported on black soldiers who were fighting enemies abroad. As blacks battled Nazi and Japanese forces, new "race riots" erupted in major cities across America.[3]

The *Pittsburgh Courier* best illustrated the role of animation in the problems the "Double V" campaign was exposing by drawing attention to a wartime reissue of the Warner Brothers cartoon *Sunday Go to Meetin' Time* (1936), which features several crude racial jokes at the expense of African Americans. The item addressing this film was one of the many articles, editorials, and letters from readers about racism in cartoons that the newspaper printed from time to time between 1944 and 1954. In the article a white army private described his reaction to viewing the cartoon while overseas in 1945. He considered it in the worst of taste and wished that the studio had instead made a picture about African American servicemen's bravery in combat.[4]

No such film was ever to come out of the cartoon studios. To be sure, animators produced images of blacks contributing to the nation's war effort, but in a manner that conformed to patriotism as understood by the animation industry. The cartoonists watered down critical and radical black political expression in order to make their caricatures of wartime blacks "safe" and thus patriotic. This political manipulation frequently resulted in their depicting African Americans of the 1940s according to the old racial stereotypes of "Jim Crow" and "Zip Coon." The artists could conceive of no other way to depict contemporary African Americans in comedic films and certainly had no live-action movie or radio comedies from which to borrow. In addition, the caricatures reflected the refusal of the federal government itself to take seriously the participation of African Americans in the war effort. By 1943 only 79,000 of the 500,000 African Americans in the U.S. Army were seeing combat; the rest were serving in segregated units overseas, performing the menial tasks of unloading ships, building roads, and driving supply convoys.[5]

Animated black servicemen similarly appeared in all-black cartoons as minstrel figures in military uniforms. Dance and music are central to their characterization. The storyboard for Walter Lantz's "Cartune" episode *Boogie Woogie Bugle Boy of Company B* (1941) calls for caricatures of black soldiers to shuffle across the floor of a tent. The music of blackface minstrelsy also shaped the presentation of African American military figures. Columbia Pictures' *Old Blackout Joe* (1942), a cartoon in which an African American air raid warden fails to darken all of the lights in his neighborhood, took its title from the minstrel song "Old Black Joe." Blackout Joe's small size reflects the condescension of the cartoonists toward the black war effort, for he looks more like a juvenile than an adult male. Echoing the insensitivity of the studio toward blacks in wartime, an exhibitor described *Old Blackout Joe* as "quite a funny cartoon. All about a little darky air-raid warden who can't get one light in particular to black out."[6]

To be sure, blackface minstrelsy also influenced war-related cartoons that did not feature African American figures. During the Civil War, minstrels had created gags involving clumsy African American soldiers incapable of accomplishing the simplest military tasks. Such ineptitude formed the basis of characterizations not only for the character Old Blackout Joe but also for Disney's Donald Duck—depicted as a soldier in films in 1942–43—and Private Snafu, Warner Brothers' white serviceman character created for government-sponsored military training cartoons. The difference between the African American and white military depictions, however, was that for every Snafu, the studios also presented a Popeye or Superman bravely fighting the Nazis and the Japanese. Even animal characters such as Bugs Bunny and Daffy Duck managed to frustrate a caricatured Adolf Hitler. Animated African American servicemen had no such heroic counterparts.

Director Bob Clampett of Leon Schlesinger Productions used African American soldier characters as means to an end. His "Merrie Melodies" episode *Coal Black an de Sebben Dwarfs* (1942) lampooned the famous tale of *Snow White* by casting garish African American figures and scoring the film with swing music. The dwarfs are seven diminutive servicemen stationed in the United States, though unlike the original seven dwarfs, they have no distinct personalities and very few lines. The plot centers on the romance between So White and Prince Chawmin and the wicked stepmother's jealousy of So White's beauty. The soldiers appear in the cartoon as "comic relief"; their military status has no relevance to the plot.

The characters in *Coal Black an de Sebben Dwarfs* speak the usual "hep" talk, as interpreted by white animators of previous films. When developing African American characters' speech patterns, the writers borrowed from the MGM "frog cartoons" of the mid-1930s, usually constructing African American characters' speech by combining stereotypical dialect, "jive" slang or scat singing, and rhymes. The script for *Coal Black an de Sebben Dwarfs* includes this passage in jive talk: "Azatee-aza-pazacezy, baza mosazy, taza-mezy. Okay, boss. Set the body down easy." Exhibitors also awkwardly blended references to minstrelsy with allusions to modern African American music. One exhibitor considered the appeal of this combination crucial to the film's success: "This is a fair color cartoon which has lots of black face jive and if your crowd can stand this, then it ought to go over."[7]

Coal Black an de Sebben Dwarfs reflects the director's fascination with black entertainment. Clampett appreciated African American music and frequently used it in films. For this particular cartoon, he sought to authenticate the music he loved by employing blacks not only to voice characters but also to play the musical score. He drew from elements of black urban culture as well; for example, the "prince" character wears a zoot suit and dances the jitterbug with So White.[8]

Clampett's directorial style worked very well in *Coal Black an de Sebben Dwarfs* with the frenetic swing music that had inspired the cartoon. Like Max Fleischer, Clampett encouraged his animators to develop their own individual styles. Unlike Fleischer, however, Clampett did not prioritize continuity. The sequences of jitterbugging African American characters nevertheless fit perfectly with the chaotic juxtapositions of clashing animation styles.

The unprecedented amount of African American sexual imagery in the film was another of Clampett's methods for visually interpreting swing. The romantic leading characters, So White and Prince Chawmin, were animation's first heterosexual African American couple to demonstrate sexual chemistry. In contrast to previous desexualized pairings of sambo male characters with "mammy" females, the zoot-suited Chawmin displays passion for the short-skirted So White by giving her kisses with the voltage of lightning bolts. For this episode Clampett hired an African American trumpeter to blow the notes that musically signified the passion of the kiss.

For all his unique ethnic imagery, Clampett could not divorce his attempt to illustrate African American swing from the stereotypes that shaped his business. The very existence of *Coal Black an de Sebben Dwarfs* depended on cultural appropriation, for the director merely did what blackface minstrels used to do—watch African Americans perform (in his case, at African American nightclubs in Los Angeles) and attempt to approximate their dancing, in his case via animation. His love of black music did not prevent him from drawing characters who sport the usual exaggerated eyes and lips. As with earlier cartoons starring black soldier figures, the servicemen in Clampett's film behave clownishly and are stationed at home instead of serving overseas. In addition, the speech of the characters, though chanted to the score's rhythm, still consists of stereotypical dialect, which the film's black actors read from the dialogue sheet approved by Clampett.

The minstrelsy-derived African American caricatures in *Coal Black an de Sebben Dwarfs* provide a stark visual contrast to the modern jazz soundtrack. Clampett illustrates swing music solely in racially generalized terms. The prince has dice for teeth—a reference to the stereotype of the African American as a crapshooter. African American servicemen are miniaturized and resemble Fats Waller or Stepin' Fetchit, thus appearing out of shape or slow-witted, respectively; similar images of inept black military troops had been a staple of blackface performance ever since the Civil War. Finally, Coal Black's vocation as a happy washerwoman made for a jazzier version of the mammy stereotype, not unlike the character in *Scrub Me Mama with a Boogie Beat.*[9]

In addition to the film's reliance on standard racial humor, *Coal Black an de Sebben Dwarfs* carried on the practice at Leon Schlesinger Productions of exploiting music owned by the distributor. As a result, the cartoon's characters serve as corporate shills. Although Warner Brothers Pictures no longer insisted that each cartoon spotlight a company-owned tune, African American musician Jimmy Lunceford's song "Blues in the Night," from the Warner film of the same name, plays during a scene in the cartoon. Studio music director Carl Stalling often used the song for scenes involving African American characters or stereotypical African American behavior. His linking of the racial identity of the composer to the racial stereotypes was part of his method of musical association; for scenes involving food, for example, he usually referred to the song "A Cup of Coffee, a Sandwich, and You." In the script for *Coal Black an de Sebben Dwarfs*, the African American female character So White cheerfully sings, "Mah hair's coal black/But mah name's So White./Ah washes all day/An' Ah got da blues in da night."[10]

Even the promotion for *Coal Black an de Sebben Dwarfs* had overtones of racial humor. Warner Brothers Pictures associated black stereotypes with black soldiers in the film's official "release sheet"—a document from a distributor describing a film to a potential exhibitor. Making the racial identity of the military figures a selling point, the sheet called the film "a dusky satire on 'Snow White'" and noted, "All of the characters are portrayed as darkies, and the seven dwarfs are all in the army." These depictions reinforced the armed forces' prejudices about African American servicemen during the war. White soldiers referred to African Americans as "apes," and military orders called them "childlike." Exhibitors would decide whether to book cartoons for their theaters on the basis of promotional materials from studios such as these release sheets. Their showing of this cartoon demonstrates their acceptance of the distributor's gross misrepresentation of African American war service and their approval of the epithets the studio used to describe its caricatures of black servicemen.[11]

The nationwide exhibitions aroused the ire of the National Association for the Advancement of Colored People. The civil rights group launched an intensive campaign against showings of *Coal Black an de Sebben Dwarfs* in April 1943. Of all the "dusky" characters in the film, the comical depictions of African American soldiers angered the organization the most. Julia Baxter of the NAACP's public relations department called the film "a decided caricature of Negro life and an insult to the race." She complained, "The production is made even more disgraceful by the fact that the 'Sebben Dwarfs' represent seven miniature Negro soldiers." Fellow member Odette Harper organized a "telephone picketing" on April 9 of many of the eighteen theaters showing the cartoon in Manhattan, the Bronx, and Brooklyn, and nineteen days later the NAACP president issued a formal protest to Warner Brothers' president Harry Warner, asking him to "take appropriate action." Warner changed nothing, however, and allowed the cartoon to continue its run.[12]

The NAACP's reasons for protesting *Coal Black and de Sebben Dwarfs* pertained to both civil rights and the U.S. war effort. The organization condemned the caricatures of African American soldiers as yet another manifestation of institutionalized racism toward African American troops. Juxtaposing the depictions with the film's patriotic symbolism, Harper observed by letter to Walter White of the NAACP: "The soldiers are subjected to indignities which are damaging to national unity. Ironically, the American flag floats over the camp in which the soldiers are quartered." Preying upon African American discontent with segregation and skepticism toward self-promotion of the United States as the defender of democracy, the Japanese did not hesitate to produce propaganda for black soldiers stationed in the Pacific, citing examples of discrimination against African Americans. To NAACP officers Baxter and Harper, *Coal Black an de Sebben Dwarfs* only gave ammunition to the enemy.[13]

The NAACP accomplished important milestones in protesting stereotypes even though it failed to get the film removed from theaters. Its activities empowered others outside the movie industry to conduct meaningful protests. Harper's picketing by telephone was important, because she was able to educate exhibitors directly about the cartoon's offensiveness. Sympathetic theater owners then had the option to boycott the film. White's contact with Warner shows that the NAACP took seriously the complaints that its national officers were receiving from members about cartoon images of African Americans. The fact that Warner Brothers Pictures never re-released this successful film despite the multiple reissues of less successful cartoons proves that the NAACP had, in the long run, achieved its goal.

The group, however, committed errors that it proceeded to repeat into the 1950s, thus sabotaging its anti-stereotype crusade. It made no contact with animation producer Leon Schlesinger or his animators—the people directly responsible for the film's content. Also, by April 1943, *Coal Black an de Sebben Dwarfs* had already been circulating through theaters for three months and had become a popular film with audiences and exhibitors, thus making Warner reluctant to withdraw it. Worst of all, the NAACP's leaders failed to express a cohesive point of view, expressing amusement at the cartoon's "jive" images while lamenting the racism of other scenes. Borrowing from the speaking style of *Amos 'n' Andy*'s characters, one of the organization's officers playfully described Prince Chawmin's car as a "super deluxe automobile."[14]

Not everyone found black urban culture as harmless as the NAACP had. Disney's only venture into African American "jive" constituted a hostile rebuke of that culture. The studio's wartime propaganda short *Spirit of '43* (1943) concerns Donald Duck's dilemma of wanting to spend money frivolously at a nightclub instead of investing in a war bond. A zoot-suited likeness of Donald represents his "evil" side, the villainous, unpatriotic antagonist discouraging him from contributing financially to an Allied victory. Disney incorporated slang into the vocabulary of the "hipster" duck, who urges Donald to gamble by shouting, "Shoot the works!" Most inflammatory, however, is the studio's association of African American culture with Nazism through the design of the nightclub, which features doors shaped like swastikas. As a negative depiction of African American life, the film marked a new low point in American animation.

In order for audiences to accept black jazz in cartoons during World War II, the studios had to associate the music with "safe" themes. Many urban African Americans and jazz artists—those who popularized the zoot suit and "jive" vocabulary—unfavorably equated war service with servitude toward whites. They decried the segregation of the armed forces, and some of them opposed military conscription. Animators, however, divorced the clothing, the slang, and the music from black political criticism and applied it to cartoon characters—including black characters—who were ready to serve their country proudly. But in doing so, the artists reduced urban black culture to its most superficial aspects.

Lantz, for example, represented jazz as a patriotic music style. In the aforementioned *Boogie Woogie Bugle Boy of Company B*, a jazz trumpeter becomes a home-front soldier, playing his bugle in a jazzy style. Perpetuating Harman-Ising's tendency to have black characters talk in rhymes, Lantz's protagonist—the musician figure Hot Breath Harry—receives a lyrical draft notice according to the film's dialogue sheet: "Little boy blue, come blow yo' horn, or we'll come an' git you as sho as yo'all is born." The "Swing Symphony" cartoon *Yankee Doodle Swing Shift* (1942), according to a *Variety* critic, was "another in series in which pop music backgrounds string of events fitting into musical buildup. Here it's a colored jive band made up of hep cats depicted as black cats. Five members go into a war factory when their band instruments are taken away for war supplies. . . . Different, and on the patriotic side."[15]

Toward the end of the war, studios altered their imagery of urban African American culture as it became part of mainstream American culture. For example, as white musicians such as Benny Goodman popularized the genre, more "swing cartoons" starred white characters. In addition, music directors for animation studios became more adept at scoring cartoons to jazz. According to Shamus Culhane, Lantz's musician Darrell Calker used his personal connections to give the "Swing Symphonies" films their sound. The only wartime cartoon to feature an African American jazz celebrity prominently was also the final cartoon to do so—the Warner Brothers "Merrie Melodies" episode *Tin Pan Alley Cats* (1943).[16]

Tin Pan Alley Cats relies on Fats Waller's personality, as interpreted by the animators, to carry the film. No caricatures of other jazz artists appear with the animated Waller—a stark contrast to the ensembles of musicians in Harman-Ising's "Happy Harmonies" and Schlesinger's own *Clean Pastures* (1937). In *Tin Pan Alley Cats*, a feline caricature of Waller bypasses religious missionaries on a city street in order to get to a nightclub. At various points the cat utters Waller's catchphrase, "What's the matter with him?" The caricature's indulgence in "wine, women, and song" mirrors Waller's similar pleasures.

Tin Pan Alley Cats recycles trends in cartooning of the mid-1930s but provides a modern jazz soundtrack for them. The cartoon resurrects Fleischer's "Betty Boop" theme of black music as exciting yet dangerous as well as the depression-era "moral cartoon" formula. The plot echoes the studio's earlier focus on church truancy in the film *Sunday Go to Meetin' Time* (1936) as Waller's caricature is tormented for his truancy from religious activity. While listening to a trumpeter's solo, he suffers a nightmarish hallucination. The characters he encounters in his dream—reused scenes from the studio's "Porky Pig" film *Porky in Wackyland* (1939)—scare the cat into leaving the club and joining the mission.

In directing this film, Bob Clampett further demonstrated his skill at manipulating images of black urbanity. In contrast to the celebration of swing culture in *Coal Black an de Sebben Dwarfs*, *Tin Pan Alley Cats* features an ominous depiction of jazz. *Tin Pan Alley Cats* also lacks the other cartoon's sexual energy, for Waller's caricature is desexualized. He has no leading lady to kiss, in contrast to the smooch shared by So White and the prince. The release of *Tin Pan Alley Cats* in July 1943 served as a hauntingly prophetic warning about Waller's lifestyle. He died of bronchial pneumonia five months later. With *Tin Pan Alley Cats*, Waller's death brought to an end the "black jazz celebrity cartoon" genre as it had existed since the days of Betty Boop.[17]

Shortly thereafter, fellow Schlesinger director Friz Freleng borrowed Clampett's idea of retelling a popular fairy tale—in this case *The Three Bears*—in blackface, but with little originality. Instead of creating unique characters like Prince Chawmin, Freleng settled for designing the bears as celebrity caricatures of Fats Waller, Stepin' Fetchit, and Andy of *Amos 'n' Andy* in the "Merrie Melodies" cartoon *Goldilocks and the Jivin' Bears* (1944). As a result, the director repeated his mistakes in *Clean Pastures* (1937) of substituting famous faces for personalities and failing to individualize the characterizations beyond visual design. He followed

Hollywood's practice of avoiding images of intact black families, making all three bears male rather than developing an African American "Papa Bear," "Mama Bear," and "Baby Bear." A human Fetchit caricature appearing as a telegram messenger significantly lacks characterization as well. The script even gives him another famous African American character's catchphrase; borrowing from a maid figure on the radio program *Fibber McGee and Molly*, the Fetchit caricature shouts, "Dat's what he said! Dat's what the man said! He said that!" Unsurprisingly, one exhibitor damned the cartoon: "Below par. Nothing to laugh at."[18]

By 1944 animators had succeeded in distancing urban black culture far from its context of wartime protest. Even rural slave figures appropriated the swing and slang of the 1940s without a hint of irony. The Terrytoons film *Eliza on the Ice* (1944) gives *Uncle Tom's Cabin* a swing twist. The cartoon, which presents Eliza's escape across the ice as a track meet and shoehorns Mighty Mouse into the story as her rescuer from Simon Legree, features a jazzy score including a verse sung by an imitator of Cab Calloway's style. The lyrics to the verse further tie slavery to black urbanity through the latter's slang: "Eliza's in the groove." By applying the once threatening urban black cultural style to a historically powerless and passive class of blacks, the Terrytoons studio ensured audience acceptance of the cultural reference. One exhibitor called the film "a good laugh-getter in this theatre."[19]

Eventually studios grew comfortable illustrating "jive" without casting any African American characters in the films. MGM's animation *The Zoot Cat* (1944) marks Hanna and Barbera's final effort to appropriate the African American culture effectively. The cartoon was their first return to "jive" since the release of *Swing Social*. Despite having built a career in animation on writing tunes such as "Preacher Song," "Jungle Rhythm," and "Pickin' Cotton," Hanna suddenly found that his talents needed to take a new direction. According to Barbera, after *Swing Social*'s failure at the box office, he and Hanna gladly resigned themselves to directing "Tom and Jerry" cartoons when the series' debut, *Puss Gets the Boot* (1940), became a hit film. For *The Zoot Cat*, however, the team found a way to give the series a "jive" twist by dressing Tom in a zoot suit to impress a female cat.[20]

The Hays Code's prohibition of interracial romance meant that Hanna and Barbera could not depict the female cat being wooed by the "zoot"

Tom as an African American. Therefore, the directors disassociated the zoot suit from its roots in urban African American culture. They used the suit to establish Tom's new hip image, in contrast to how "corny" the female cat had found him before he put on the suit. The film's setting was a suburban home instead of Harlem. In addition, the script described the female kitten as "the young college type that is plenty hep." In the script the rhyming speech usually reserved for black characters became "jive talk" for the kitten, who calls the pre-zoot Tom "a square at the fair" and "a goon from Saskatoon." Clearly by 1944 African American culture had extended beyond African Americans and become familiar enough for studios to parody successfully by reducing it to a matter of flashy clothes and slang.[21]

The Zoot Cat ironically used older African American music to shape Tom's new "zoot" persona. Borrowing a tactic employed by the Fleischer brothers a decade earlier for "Betty Boop" episodes, Hanna and Barbera constructed much of the dialogue in *The Zoot Cat* from the titles of Cab Calloway's songs. While wooing a female cat, for example, Tom romantically announces, "When I am with you, I am what you call a hep cat. I am hep to the jive." In another scene, Tom, when asked to dance, replies, "Well all reet, well all root, well all right," in what the script calls a "jivy voice." The lines refer to Calloway's 1930s hits "Are You All Reet" and "Are You Hep to the Jive." While derivative, the dialogue is at least more intelligible than *Swing Social*'s "Nick nocks, Tom deco—kromo stava tava tae tae."[22]

As World War II drew to a close, animators turned from images of zoot-suited figures and black soldier caricatures toward the rural caricatures of old. But the war context enabled anti-stereotype activists to reject those figures, too. The *Pittsburgh Courier* reported that a theater in Los Angeles had paired a documentary on African Americans—*Americans All*—with the Schlesinger cartoon *Angel Puss* (1944), which features a sambo figure. Many viewers complained that the exhibitor should not have shown the cartoon on the same bill with the documentary, which calls for an end to racism and prejudice. The head of the Screen Cartoonists Guild told the *Courier* that some of the local's members also resented having to make cartoons that engaged in racial caricature.[23]

Both the newspaper and the cartoon's distributor—Warner Brothers Pictures—took the matter seriously. The periodical contacted the cartoon studio itself and complained directly to the artists about the offensiveness of the sambo. The studio responded but claimed that it was blameless for *Angel Puss*. Producer Edward Selzer noted that Schlesinger had made the cartoon before selling his studio to the distributor. The new studio, now Warner Brothers Cartoons, though retaining most of Schlesinger's staff, had had nothing to do with the production of *Angel Puss*. Nevertheless, Selzer's refusal to admit fault signaled a new reluctance to be associated publicly with allegations of racism. Never before had the animation industry expressed such concern.[24]

The *Pittsburgh Courier* capitalized on its budding relationship with the animation industry. In October 1944 the paper reported on correspondence from the Hollywood Screen Cartoon Producers' association (HSCP), indicating that the group "planned to seriously consider at an executive meeting . . . the subject of harmful caricatures of minority races of American citizens." The organization's president, Walter Lantz, who only three years earlier had identified the majority of a cartoon's black characters as "niggers," requested "a specific letter" from activists containing a "suggested plan of correction." In addition to Lantz, the article identified Walt Disney and the cartoon studios MGM, Famous Studios, Warner Brothers (recently bought by the distributor from Leon Schlesinger), Terrytoons, and Screen Gems (Columbia Pictures' animation department) as members of the association. It looked as though the activists had achieved a major step toward eliminating stereotypes by educating the animation producers about problematic images in their films and receiving pledges of their cooperation.[25]

Signs of progress were short-lived, however, as the relationship between the black press and the animation industry soon collapsed. Lantz was the most committed to the HSCP's promise to the newspaper; he never produced a film starring African American characters after that year's "Swing Symphony" episode *Jungle Jive* (1944). Most of the other producers decided against making significant changes in representing African Americans. Paramount's Famous Studio, MGM, and Warner Brothers continued to use traditional images such as blackface, Stepin Fetchit caricatures, and mammy characters for another ten years. The *Courier*, meanwhile, did not further press its members to end the stereotyping but instead cited milestones of progress such as producer George Pal's announcement of Duke

Ellington's planned appearance in the cartoon *Date with Duke* over a year before its release in 1947.[26]

Still, the activists had gained important ground by 1945. Animators were no longer diluting the politics of black protest, and they were now aware that even the old rural stereotypes had become political. Even so, the artists received few complaints when they continued to caricature blacks in an unflattering manner. As the next chapter shows, the cartoonists were defying not only the protesters but the nation's changing racial climate as well by persisting in the production of black stereotypes.

SIX

African American Representation and Changing Race Relations

As World War II ended, the movie industry offered fewer roles for African Americans. The popularity of the all-black musical had waned. Because of mounting criticism from civil rights activists about servile characters played by blacks, roles for maid and butler characters in movies dried up. Meanwhile, leading roles for African Americans in dramatic films were few and far between.

The animated theatrical cartoon was one of the few media that remained consistent in its African American imagery. Hollywood had not developed any new black comedy stars during the war. Therefore, animators continued to draw on older actors and characterizations for their cartoons. The studios had not received many complaints from exhibitors or viewers regarding the persistence of the hoary stereotypes. Moreover, the animated sambos, mammies, and other black figures provided steady work for a few black actors during these lean years for African Americans in Hollywood.

The sambo figure was the first of the African American characterizations to become the focus of heavy criticism after the war. Jasper, the star of George Pal's "Puppetoons" series for Paramount, came under attack by the black press in 1946. For all his visual creativity in the use of pixillation, Pal continued to base a significant portion of the humor in Jasper's films on conversations in the dialect of blackface minstrels. People complained to the point where *Ebony* magazine reported that the episodes "have been criticized by Negro and white newspapers, organizations, and notables as perpetuating the myth of Negro shiftlessness, fear, and childishness."[1]

Pal answered charges of racism by claiming that he was only replicating characterizations that had existed in American culture for years. He said that his enjoyment of American folklore naturally led him to adapt the sambo to animation. To be sure, Jasper's episodes are on a par with contemporary sambo films from other studios, such as Leon Schlesinger's *Flop Goes the Weasel* and *Angel Puss*, which also feature rural settings and characters talking "in dialect." Many of Pal's films starring white characters, however, came not from folklore but rather from literary works. The same care he put into transforming these white characters from the printed page into strong animated figures did not extend to the stars of the "Jasper" cartoons. [2]

Stung by the criticism, Pal once again drew from African American folklore, this time for a film about a strong black adult male—the antithesis of the sambo. *John Henry and the Inky-Poo* (1946) brought to animation traditional work songs and ballads about a steel-driving man. As early as 1909 Louise Bascom published a song with a two-line refrain: "Johnie Henry was a hard-workin' man,/He died with the hammer in his hand." Pal remained relatively faithful to the songs, animating John Henry as a muscular blue-collar laborer with a booming voice. His outperforming of a steel-driving machine (the Inky-Poo) gives him a superhuman quality that distinguishes him from Jasper as well as the mumbling, scrawny Stepin' Fetchit caricatures of black men that were standard at the time. [3]

In contrast to its condemnation of Jasper, *Ebony* romanticized Pal's film about John Henry. The magazine declared that *John Henry and the Inky-Poo* contained "no Negro stereotypes"—a claim that ignores several examples of conventional (and stereotypical) black representation in the film. Stephen Foster's minstrel song "De Camptown Ladies" plays while John prepares to compete against the Inky-Poo machine on the railroad, and the narrator refers to John's mother as "his mammy." In addition, Pal conformed to contemporary movie depictions of African American domestic life, which did not show intact African American families but rather portrayed households headed solely by mothers. Moreover, Pal's depiction of John Henry contradicts various folk ballads, which give him a wife (identified variously as Polly Ann, Julie Ann, Mary Ann, or Lucy), a father, and/or a son. [4]

Pal's blend of radical black heroic imagery with Hollywood racial conventions in *John Henry and the Inky-Poo* was successful. In addition to drawing favorable reviews from the press, the film received an Academy Award nomination for best cartoon short subject of 1946. In a sense, the Academy of Motion Picture Arts and Sciences was rewarding Pal's attempt to break away from the conventional clownish black figures. More important, however, the award validated the emergence of strong and mild-mannered African American characters, sending the message that animators need not stereotype blacks in order to produce a popular cartoon.

The animation industry did not immediately heed the message; sambo characters persisted for a few more years. Paramount released new "Jasper" cartoons through 1947. That same year Warner Brothers distributed yet another sambo cartoon directed by Chuck Jones and starring the African boy figure Inki. Exhibitors and audiences still enjoyed the cartoons, and distributors and studios suffered no repercussions for offering them.

Nevertheless, now that Pal had produced an alternative black male image, activists grew increasingly intolerant of animated sambos. In 1949 the NAACP challenged the reissue of Ub Iwerks's 1935 cartoon *Little Black Sambo*. By that time Castle Films had acquired the rights to sell prints of the cartoon for viewing at home. Macy's department store became an outlet for sales of the film. Reissued, it carried African American imagery of the Great Depression into the postwar era. Moreover, the NAACP objected that the film's distributor and retailer were marketing the outdated stereotypes to juvenile audiences.

The NAACP's campaign to have the film removed from Macy's went surprisingly smoothly. Taking a strong stance, the organization offered no compromises. Upon discovering Macy's advertisement for the cartoon, NAACP administrative assistant Madison Jones contacted the store and requested that the film be withdrawn from sale. He lambasted *Little Black Sambo* as "derogatory and offensive to Negroes" and "a picturization and caricature of Negroes in a most gross and exaggerated sense." He warned: "Such a film, which is especially sold for the entertainment of children of tender age, perpetrates harm of the gravest kind. Whatever entertainment value the film may have is thoroughly negated by the depiction of the Negro caricature." Macy's was prompt to cooperate with the organization. Responding to Jones by letter a few weeks later, H. Norman Neubert, the store's public relations manager, announced the company's decision "to withdraw the film from sale at Macy's."[5]

The NAACP had a more difficult time persuading Castle Films to stop distributing the film to stores. The parties disagreed on the nature of the cartoon's stereotypes. Jones wrote to the distribution company, requesting that it stop selling *Little Black Sambo*. The company's spokesman, seeing only the brown skin color as potentially offensive, offered to eliminate color prints of the film, saying, "I would like very much to show you the black and white edition of the picture as I do not believe that this is objectionable." The distributors considered only the Technicolor Sambo racist, not his black and white counterpart, and failed to acknowledge altogether the mammy characterization of Sambo's mother or the stereotypical dialect as problematic for African American audiences.[6]

Still, the NAACP set a precedent by making the sambo characterization unprofitable. This was quite an accomplishment, for the image had been an extremely successful one for animators. For producers such as Pat Sullivan and George Pal, sambos were their only major stars. The image had appeared in pioneering cartoons such as Sullivan's silent "Sammy Johnsin" episodes, Chuck Jones's radically stylized works, and Pal's puppet animation films. Nevertheless, after Jones directed one last "Inki" cartoon in 1951, studios produced no new sambo cartoons.

Southern black figures also became a liability after World War II. Animation and live-action studios had trouble justifying the old stereotypical images in light of the racism of the "Jim Crow" South. Many African American veterans returned from the war determined to end racial segregation in the United States. In the South many of them attempted to register to vote and challenged prohibitions against their efforts. They spearheaded boycotts against businesses that segregated patrons. They even testified at a hearing in Mississippi in which the NAACP sought to have the Senate remove the state's rabidly segregationist senator Theodore Bilbo from office for disenfranchising blacks. These public campaigns clashed with Hollywood's current images of happy, shuffling plantation workers.[7]

Many new films set in the South overlooked references to slavery even as they promoted the image of American democracy and leadership of the free world. The MGM cartoon *Uncle Tom's Cabana* (1947), for example, tried to draw humor from Stowe's novel without calling attention to Uncle Tom's enslavement. Adapting the story to the present, director Fred "Tex" Avery depicted Legree as the owner of all the buildings in a city except for Uncle Tom's log cabin. Instead of purchasing Tom, however, Legree threatens to foreclose on his home. The old images of the South—plantations,

cotton fields, and slaves' shacks—appear in the film, and the film's credits
are superimposed over what the script describes as a "shot of old southern
mansion, pan to little cabin in cotton." For one visual gag featuring the
ramshackle cabin surrounded by urban skyscrapers, the script calls for a
"medium shot of Uncle Tom hoeing cotton in front of cabin." This shot
sums up what a struggle it was for animators to fit black characters—long
conceived in a rural antebellum context—into cartoons set in contemporary American society.[8]

Avery's interpretation of the Uncle Tom character was in part revolutionary because of its somewhat sexual nature. The film was Hollywood's
first adaptation of Stowe's novel to refrain from depicting Uncle Tom as a
desexualized, maternal figure caring for his owner's daughter, Little Eva.
Animated black characters had not expressed themselves sexually since
Coal Black an de Sebben Dwarfs in 1943. *Uncle Tom's Cabana,* however,
flirts with violating the Code's prohibition on depicting miscegenation.
Recalling the imagery of Fleischer's "Betty Boop" jazz episodes, the cartoon is constructed around Legree's lust for a shapely adult Little Eva. But
Uncle Tom himself contributes to the film's sexual humor in a rare disclo-
sure of interracial lust. After Tom describes Little Eva's luxurious home, he
remarks, "And dat ain't all she got, neither," as she appears on the screen.
Nevertheless, *Uncle Tom's Cabana* insists in no uncertain terms that Uncle
Tom and Little Eva have a strictly platonic relationship. When introducing
her, he calls her "mah only friend." In addition, the film gives her more so-
cioeconomic power than it gives to him, reflecting the economic reality of
the day. The plot depicts Tom as dependent on Eva in that he needs her to
sing at his nightclub so he can raise money for the mortgage on his cabin.
He refers to her as his "last hope."[9]

Despite this dependence, Uncle Tom in *Uncle Tom's Cabana* demonstrates a strength that African American characters had rarely possessed
since the 1930 cartoon *Dixie Days*. In both cartoons Uncle Tom physically
defeats Legree. Unlike Legree's mere whipping of Tom in the earlier film,
the violence that Legree inflicts on him in Avery's cartoon exemplifies the
animation industry's dependence on gags involving guns and explosives.
The script for *Uncle Tom's Cabana* associates Uncle Tom with World War
II imagery by having him tell of Legree's attacks with "dem rocket guns,
'n dive bombers, 'n bazookas, 'n dem Japs runnin' all over da place." Tom's

claim of having encountered "Japs" is significant, given that no cartoon released or written during the war discusses or shows African American characters fighting the Japanese or other military enemies. His remark therefore represents an improvement over previous African American cartoon clowns like the "little darky air raid warden" in Columbia Pictures' *Old Blackout Joe* (1942). Movie audiences would never have the opportunity to hear of Tom's battles against enemy forces in *Uncle Tom's Cabana*, however, since MGM deleted the reference to the "Japs" from the film before its July 1947 release—two years after the conclusion of the war.[10]

In 1948 the Supreme Court decided that a distributor must release each film—feature, short subject, or newsreel—individually to exhibitors. As a result, distributors lost much of their investments in cartoons when exhibitors refused to pay separate fees for both a feature and a short subject, since the cost for a patron to see a feature was the same with or without a cartoon. To offset the rising costs of animation, distributors began reissuing old cartoons. These films often earned only slightly less money than new releases, without having to cover the production costs of a new cartoon. In place of the modernized black hero of *Uncle Tom's Cabana*, older slave and sharecropper images returned to theaters. Many of the reissues starring crude rural black figures attracted the attention of the NAACP. Walter Lantz's *Scrub Me Mama with a Boogie Beat* (1941), with its cast of southern black characters the producer had described as "niggers," was one such reissue in 1948.

As with the NAACP's protest of *Coal Black an de Sebben Dwarfs*, the organization's interoffice correspondence about the reissue of *Scrub Me Mama with a Boogie Beat* reveals that the officers considered the racial stereotypes problematic but had trouble taking them completely seriously. Edna Kerin described the offensive images in a memo, then complained of the cartoon, "Incidentally, it isn't at all funny—which voids its purpose as a cartoon." And while Julia Baxter perceptively lamented the dramatically different depictions of Northern and Southern African Americans, she referred to the singing African American Northerner as a "smooth, high yaller from Harlem." NAACP officials accordingly experienced difficulty in persuading others of the graveness of their concerns.[11]

An executive of Universal Pictures capitalized on the weaknesses of the NAACP's campaign. In a meeting with the group's public relations department officers, E. L. McEvoy offered valid reasons for his reluctance to pull *Scrub Me Mama with a Boogie Beat* from theaters. He noted that the closing of Lantz's studio had forced Universal to release older films and that the cartoon's successful initial run had prompted Universal to reissue it. He could not recall complaints from anyone regarding the film's content in the seven years of its existence. He told the officials that Universal had already contracted with exhibitors to distribute the cartoon—underlining the problem with the NAACP's reactive approach. Most important, he hit upon a major weakness of the NAACP campaign, what Thomas Cripps has described as its insensitivity toward African American actors. McEvoy warned that the group's activism could result in the disappearance of roles for these performers.[12]

Internal memoranda at the NAACP document the points of vulnerability in McEvoy's argument. He did not deny the existence of the film's stereotypes but excused them as typical of Hollywood filmmaking by offering his own examples of using ethnic slurs in the workplace. He had specifically asked for only the white NAACP officer's opinion about the cartoon, although that member had been working as the group's public relations assistant for less than two months. He had demonstrated ethnic insensitivity by referring to African Americans as "niggers." When it relayed the proceedings of the meeting with McEvoy to the Jewish Labor Committee (JLC), the NAACP gained a new ally.[13]

The JLC contributed significantly to the NAACP's campaign against Universal. The committee accomplished more between January and February 1949—when Universal withdrew *Scrub Me Mama*—than the NAACP had over the three previous months. On December 28 Madison Jones of the NAACP wrote to the JLC's assistant field director, Emanuel Muravchik, asking the group to "contact Universal and go on record as being against this type of motion picture." A week later, on January 3, field director Irving Salert expressed his desire to work with the NAACP toward getting not only "an apology from the Universal Film Corporation" but also "a withdrawing of the film by the Universal Picture outfit." Universal took the JLC's criticism more seriously than it had that of the NAACP. In February 1949, according to Jones, "the Jewish Labor Committee in California brought [the matter] to the attention of executives of Universal in Hollywood and the picture was taken out of circulation." By contacting the Hollywood elite, the JLC had not done anything differently than the NAACP; but the quick response from the moguls shows that the JLC possessed more power than the NAACP in the movie industry.[14]

The protest against *Scrub Me Mama* served as a steppingstone for the coalition to take on larger issues. The two groups continued to work together on various campaigns, but the JLC left the question of animated black caricatures to the NAACP to tackle alone, thus destroying the most effective force that anti-stereotype activists had possessed in removing cartoons from theaters. In an interview Muravchik noted that animated films "wouldn't [have been] important in our agenda." He considered them "way down on the list" of the JLC's priorities. The subject of cartoons in general "may not have come up in joint meetings" with the NAACP.[15]

After Universal withdrew the cartoon, the days of "Jim Crow" animation were numbered. No studio made new cartoons starring rural black characters. To be sure, cartoonists still portrayed Southern blacks as lazy and easygoing but did not give them brown skin or large lips anymore. Cartoons lampooning the Civil War era featured Union and Confederate soldiers, and animated films set in the modern South exclusively starred white "hillbilly" stereotypes. There was, however, still one important racial difference in terms of characterization: neither the soldiers nor the hillbillies were laborers and thus never picked cotton or washed clothes in their cartoons.

The mammy figure survived into the 1950s—largely thanks to MGM, whose filmmakers found that the character could be adapted to the suburban consumerism of the decade without changing her behavior. Employment of a domestic laborer was a sign of affluence for whites, and many white housewives spent the earnings of their breadwinning husbands on domestic goods and hired African American women as domestic workers to operate those goods. MGM's "colored maid" character in the "Tom and Jerry" series may have handled new tasks in the postwar cartoons, but she possessed the traditional attributes of the mammy characterization—obesity, Negro dialect, ragged clothing, and servility.[16]

Radio had a profound influence on the development of the mammy character in animated films. Mammies in cartoons of the late 1940s began to exhibit traits of the title character of the radio comedy *Beulah*, a very popular fictional maid who laughed at her employer's worst jokes and sighed, "Love dat man." Three years after Beulah's first appearance in 1944 (on another radio show, *Fibber McGee and Molly*), MGM resurrected its "colored maid" character—last seen in *The Lonesome Mouse* (1943)—and adapted her to Beulah's personality. The script for *Old Rockin' Chair Tom* (1948) features a variation on Beulah's catchphrase: "The maid chuckles and says, 'Heh, heh, love dat cat.'" After 1947 MGM's "colored maid" figure became more jovial, often joking with Tom Cat. Her use of the catchphrase exposes her blankness as a cartoon character; having debuted in 1940, she was now reduced to speaking a newer character's famous signature line in order to shore up her own mammy characterization.[17]

Hanna and Barbera still defined the mammy figure through traditional ethnic generalizations and refused to give her an identity of her own. She retained her apron, reinforced stockings, and house slippers. She continued to be depicted with a heavyset figure and her face unseen off-screen. The studio had not yet even named her in scripts and dialogue sheets, although scripts now referred to "the cat" and "the little mouse" as "Tom" and "Jerry." Nine years after the script for *Handle with Care*, a 1948 dialogue sheet for *Saturday Evening Puss* still identified the character as "colored maid." Her actions merely reflected stereotypes, as demonstrated in the opening scene from the script for *A Mouse in the House* (1947): "Maid shuffles into scene, and winds clock."[18]

Remarkably, MGM wrote the mammy's stereotyped dialogue in exactly the same manner throughout her eleven-year run in the "Tom and Jerry" series. The studio continued to express her lines in misspelled words and ungrammatical syntax. In December 1948 the script for *The Framed Cat* provided instruction on how to emphasize the mispronounced words: "She calls frantically to Tom, 'Thomas, come in an' git diss chicken-stealin' mouse.' She accents 'git' and 'diss' by pointing." Nine years earlier, both "git" and "diss" had appeared in the script for her very first cartoon, *Handle with Care*. One sentence in the *Part Time Pal* (1947) script contains two incorrectly conjugated verbs: "Fade in on Maid, lecturing Tom, saying 'either you keeps dat mouse outta dat icebox, or you goes out!'"[19]

MGM's colored maid was both a traditional racial stereotype and a signifier for African American second-class citizenship in the postwar United States. Her wardrobe remained consistent with that of mammies in earlier works of American literature but was a far cry from the clothing of post–

World War II suburban women. As white-collar male characters, Elmer Fudd and Goofy sported gray suits and bowties, lived in affluent neighborhoods, and referred to work at "the office"; female characters like Famous Studios' Olive Oyl wore long dresses or skirts and high-heeled shoes and portrayed homemakers. By contrast, the costume of MGM's mammy, like the domestic work that she performed, denoted the character's lack of affluence. By wearing the traditional mammy clothes of antebellum literature, she represented African Americans' persistent social inequality since the pre–Civil War era. By working as a maid, she signified the need of the African American family, unlike the white family, for income from the woman's domestic service. Housewives were figured as white; cartoons never showed African American housewives.

Hanna and Barbera refused to allow the role of the mammy in the "Tom and Jerry" series to evolve. She continued to appear mostly in the opening and closing scenes of films in order to establish the plot and then bring it to a conclusion. The studio did devise new variations on her attempts to keep the house clean and mouse-free. In cartoons from 1940 to 1943, she had merely told Tom to catch Jerry or to stop breaking dishes and then kicked Tom out of the house. In cartoons of the late 1940s and early 1950s, she occasionally ventured away from the house and introduced new characters. In the dialogue sheet for *Sittin' Kitten*, the working title for the film *Triplet Trouble* (1952), she warns Tom, "If you don't take good care of dose little angels here while I's gone, I'll pulverize you to pieces—you hear me?" The script for *Cat of Tomorrow*—later released as the maid's finale, *Push-Button Kitty* (1952)—calls for the maid to introduce a robot to take Tom's place:

> (Scene 7) The maid is heard calling, "Thomas, oh Thomas, come in here and see what I'se got." . . .
> (Scene 10) Tom laughs and swings his arm to the wall, then swishes his arm, belittling the mechanical cat. The maid says to Tom, "Is you through laughin', Tom? Den watch diss."[20]

The maid signifies the subhuman in some of her appearances. Though irritated by Tom's failure to catch Jerry, she acknowledges her inability to get rid of the mouse by herself and expresses thanks whenever Tom helps her. Her fear of Jerry and dependence on Tom are not new character traits, having first appeared in *The Lonesome Mouse*. The script for *Old Rockin'* *Chair Tom*, however, gives her an unusual emotional intensity by having her weep and pine for Tom: "The maid sobs and clasps her hands as she cries, 'Oh, if Thomas was only here—Thomas!'" Although Tom demonstrates loyalty to the servant by rescuing her, even striking a "dramatic 'I shall save her' pose," according to the script, the relationship between them evolves into that of proud master (Tom) and humbled servant (maid) in the film's dialogue sheet: "(Maid sincere—overemphasizes—) 'And I sincerely hopes you will accept mah apologies *an'* diss small token of gratitude.'" [21]

Tom occasionally possesses an awareness of the servile nature of the maid's labor. Most of the cartoons depict him as a pet under the maid's command. Hanna and Barbera, however, give Tom more human qualities after the war, such as walking on two legs instead of four. He also exhibits more human behavior, some of which is condescending toward the maid. In *Part Time Pal* an intoxicated Tom expects her to bring him a meal at the kitchen table. In the script the cat "ties table cloth around his own neck, hicks daintily, and rings bell. He waits, vexed, and then bangs bell violently." Becoming impatient, he "stalks to stairs, and gives weak whistle for maid. Then bangs bannister with umbrella. Whistles loudly for maid." In the script for *Cat of Tomorrow*, Tom does not demand service but rather allows the maid to work around him, for which she sarcastically expresses appreciation: "Pan in on Tom lying on a pillow with his eyes closed, swinging his leg up in the air as the maid sweeps under his raised leg. She says, 'Sorry to disturb you, Mr. Thomas.' Then she sweeps under his other leg and says, 'Thank you so much.'"[22]

Cat of Tomorrow also uses the mammy to combine references to postwar consumerism with older ethnic generalizations regarding faithfulness as well as attitudes toward technology. After Tom catches a mouse that a robot cat failed to catch, the maid declares, "Boy dey can have their newfangled mechanos—all I want is a plain old-fashioned cat." Her mishaps with the robot reinforce the myth of black technical incompetence. Yet by preferring Tom to the robot, she also epitomizes the "faithful servant" stereotype. Her purchase of the mechanical cat in order to keep her employer's home clean satirizes the postwar trend of white women hiring African American domestics to clean their homes with their new appliances.[23]

The mammy figure participates in the violent scenes of several postwar episodes to a greater degree than in the wartime films. The gags in "Tom and Jerry" involve more explosions and more striking of characters over the head with objects in the late 1940s and early 1950s than in the films released between 1940 and 1943. The maid occasionally inflicts the violence—a unique development because female cartoon characters rarely exhibit physical aggression. The script for *Part Time Pal* states: "Maid out with broom and smacks Tom on head. . . . Maid jumps and yells, 'Bombs Away.' Big explosion, and Jerry cowers." She also receives painful blows to the body in some cartoons. The script for *A Mouse in the House* notes, "Maid reaches bottom of stairs just as Butch and Tom tear out, and accidentally bang her with their frying pan and coal scuttle." Comparisons of similar gags in different cartoons illustrate the increased intensity of violence. In both *The Lonesome Mouse* (1943) and *Old Rockin' Chair Tom* (1948), Jerry Mouse snaps the maid's garter. The earlier cartoon's script provides a detailed description of the gag: "This time he pulls the maid's stocking hand over hand and her garter is pulled into the scene, attached to the stocking. The little mouse lets go of the stocking and the garter splats her leg hard." The script for the later cartoon, in contrast, emphasizes the impact of the blow: "Jerry . . . grabs the maid's stocking, stretching her garter and then lets it go, snapping her leg with a 'BAM.'"[24]

The maid's expanded dialogue was both a creative and an economic development in the "Tom and Jerry" series. She did not appear as frequently after the war as she had during it. Many new talking supporting characters such as Spike Bulldog and Nibbles Mouse provided dialogue that established plots for films set outside the home, while the maid's employment at the residence restricted her from participating in cartoons set beyond the kitchen or living room. Also, as a result of shrinking budgets plaguing the animation industry, cartoon characters began to move less and talk more. Since Tom and Jerry were mute characters, their loquacious co-stars appeared more frequently. The maid now had more to say—often wisecracks and asides—in her brief scenes than in the earlier cartoons. The dialogue sheet for *Old Rockin' Chair Tom* contains this complaint to Tom: "Da trouble wid you is you is getting' too old ta catch mice." In the dialogue sheet for *Polka Dot Puss*, she warns herself, "Lan sakes—If I stan here in da open door like dis I'm gonna catch my death o'cold."[25]

The African American actress Lillian Randolph, the only voice of the durable character, kept her job in spite of complaints from anti-stereotype activists. She had built her career on the mammy characterization. While voicing the mammy for "Tom and Jerry," she played a similar character on the radio show *The Great Gildersleeve*, and she also played the title role in *Beulah* briefly in the early 1950s. She valued the benefits that the parts brought to her career and fought staunchly to protect the availability of such roles from the efforts of people whose protests of these character-izations in film and radio threatened her livelihood. While lamenting a resolution by the American Federation of Radio Artists that called for an end to racist African American roles, she declared: "I am very proud that I can portray a stereotyped role. When you take that away from me you take away my birthright." She also commented on the futility of the protests: "Such things as that should be left alone. There are certain traditions we can't get rid of." Like many other black actors, she blamed groups such as the American Federation of Television and Radio Actors and the NAACP for the mass unemployment of black performers. Indeed, they influenced Hollywood's phasing out of servile black characters but did not urge stu-dios to develop less stereotypical roles. In her frustration she questioned the credibility of Walter White, the leader of the NAACP, on the basis of his light skin, saying that he "was only 1/8 Negro and not qualified to speak for Negroes."[26]

Despite Randolph's barbs, the activists continued to target the "Tom and Jerry" maid. In addition, the NAACP argued that her cartoons harmed ju-venile audiences. Protesting the 1949 reissue of *The Lonesome Mouse* (1943), Richard O. Riess—president of the University of Rochester's branch of the NAACP—lamented to White, "These cartoons are being shown mostly to young, impressionable minds," adding: "The prejudice which is conveyed in these cartoons is subtle, but nevertheless vicious, to the innocent mind. You might say that it enters the 'back door of their minds.'" Riess had a valid point. The cartoons were certainly popular with young audiences. Months earlier, exhibitor Fred Weppler had written about showing *The Lonesome Mouse*, "Played this one in a cartoon festival and when Tom and Jerry flashed on the screen, the kids brought the house down."[27]

The business generated by the "Tom and Jerry" series through the late 1940s and early 1950s made MGM reluctant to capitulate to the NAACP.

Cartoons starring the mammy character still received positive reviews. As a result, exhibitors continued to rent them. In 1953 exhibitor Ray McFarlane wrote of the mammy's final cartoon, *Push-Button Kitty* (1952), "Tom and Jerry cartoons are all good, but we had more than the usual number of good comments on this one." Not surprisingly, then, by July 1950, nine months after the first memorandum on *The Lonesome Mouse*, Madison Jones admitted to Riess that despite the NAACP's efforts toward having the cartoon withdrawn, "we did not get very far."[28]

The group's campaign against the film was not helped by similar efforts from a man with communist affiliations. On October 31, 1949, Edna Kerin, an assistant in the NAACP's public relations department, noted that a man named Sam Friedbaum had complained about the "Tom and Jerry" cartoon *The Lonesome Mouse* to his union—the United Office and Professional Workers of America (UOPWA)—and that the union planned to send "a press release to the *Post*, *Compass* and *Daily Worker* on the subject." The UOPWA membership was heavily communist, and the union may have had communist leadership. Reflecting the NAACP's aversion to communism, the group's papers do not include any correspondence about the film with Friedbaum or the UOPWA or from the union to the newspapers. Even if the NAACP had been willing to join forces, the UOPWA would have made a powerless ally. By the time Kerin wrote her memo, the Congress of Industrial Organizations had charged the UOPWA with allowing communist concerns to prohibit effective organizing. A year later, in 1950, it was expelled from the CIO.[29]

Nevertheless, the activism had some effect. Hanna and Barbera never used the maid character again after MGM released *Push-Button Kitty* in September 1952. Lillian Randolph ended her vocal work as the maid on "Tom and Jerry" while starting a new role in the television series *Amos 'n' Andy*. Instead of replacing her with another actor, Hanna and Barbera decided to replace the character altogether with a bland married white couple. No other studio used the characterization either after 1952. The animation industry, in effect, had "fired" her.[30]

Another black figure that animators struggled to adapt to postwar culture was the jazz musician. The newest jazz craze was bebop, and the subdued, introverted style of its performers was a departure from the exaggerated, comical facial expressions and dance moves of swing artists. As a result, animation studios were left without any funny gestures or catchphrases on which to base jokes; no studio made caricatures out of Kenny Clarke, Charlie Parker, or Thelonious Monk. Only the maverick studio UPA tried to animate to the music, hiring African American musician Phil Moore to score *Rooty Toot Toot* (1952), a cartoon about a love triangle among white characters. The film's director, John Hubley, later boasted that the cartoon was the first with a score by an African American musician. For its efforts UPA received an Academy Award nomination for the picture that year.[31]

Ignoring the emergence of bebop, music directors at animation studios regularly scored cartoons with swing music during the last years of the war. Swing had become more popular with audiences, and studios no longer felt compelled to use the music only for films starring black cartoon characters. For example, MGM's Tom Cat serenaded a female cat with Louis Jordan's "Is You Is or Is You Ain't My Baby" in the "Tom and Jerry" film *Solid Serenade* (1946), whose story synopsis refers to Tom's musical number as "a bit of jive." The brassiness of the music suited violent cartoon action better than the more relaxed bebop style. Moreover, swing had a sweeter sound and a cleaner, more predictable rhythm than bebop's irregular harmonizing, timing, and meter.[32]

Animators gradually decreased their caricaturing of urban blacks while using more animals and white characters. In 1945 Universal terminated the "Swing Symphonies" series, which had cast African American figures almost exclusively to complement swing soundtracks. In addition, studios distanced the few images of the zoot suit in postwar cartoons from its original context of African American protest. The Famous Studios cartoon *Jitterbug Jive* (1950) focuses on two white sailors—Popeye and Bluto—trying to "outjive" each other for Olive Oyl's affections. The sailor characters ironically wear zoot suits, the clothing style that had made black youths the targets of servicemen in Los Angeles's "Zoot Suit Riot" seven years earlier.[33]

Famous Studios associated jazz with black servitude even after World War II. In 1947 the company created Buzzy the Crow, so named because of Jackson Beck's approximation of black comedian Eddie "Rochester" Anderson's buzz saw voice. Unlike Stepin' Fetchit—a shuffling figure with his head bending low—Buzzy struts, brags about being clever, and sings swing songs. In addition, in each episode he successfully outwits a cat named Katnip, not unlike Anderson delivering sarcastic backtalk to his white boss, played on the radio by Jack Benny on *The Jack Benny Show*. Buzzy's besting of the cat was a risky idea, since many white listeners found Anderson's character too impudent and lacking humility when insulting Benny. The studio tempered Buzzy's unusual aggressiveness and cleverness with the traditional African American stereotypes of servility and language. The crow calls the cat "Boss," the title Anderson gave Benny. In each cartoon Buzzy satirically caters to Katnip, giving him phony alternatives to recipes or instructions that call for the use of crow meat. Also, Buzzy speaks in the typical racial dialect, uttering lines like "You is absotively right," thus appearing less educated than the cat.[34]

Buzzy's aggressive behavior reflects the loosening enforcement by the PCA against violent images in films. In general, cartoons from Famous Studios are some of the most violent animated films produced during the postwar era. As a result, Buzzy shows more physical agency than most African American characters in the beatings, gunshots, and explosions that he inflicts on Katnip Cat. The crow is a "trickster" character from the slave folktale tradition, not unlike Br'er Rabbit when tricking the vulnerable Miss Cow in *Uncle Remus;* his gratuitous and sadistic violence leaves little room for sentimentality. In *No Ifs, Ands or Butts* (1954), Buzzy drops a two-ton weight on the cat, hands him a lit firecracker, and fires a pistol at his teeth.[35]

Buzzy's buzz saw voice, repetitive plots, and violent antics did little to win over audiences. He starred in at most two films per year between 1947 and 1954; in comparison, the studio's seven or eight annual "Popeye" or "Casper the Friendly Ghost" episodes. He was only one of several recurring "Noveltoons" characters, including the precocious Little Audrey and the slow-witted, enormous infant Baby Huey. Years after Famous dropped Buzzy, he had not even left an impression on the people involved in the production of his cartoons. Neither Jackson Beck (who voiced Buzzy) nor Syd Raymond (who voiced Katnip) remembered the bird when asked for anecdotes. Beck had forgotten having done the voice of Buzzy.[36]

In the 1950s the NAACP turned its attention to offensive television situation comedies. The organization was preoccupied with protesting television adaptations of the radio series *Amos 'n' Andy* and *Beulah*. Although the negative publicity eventually led to cancellation of the programs by 1953, the anti-cartoon activism of the organization suffered. As the 1950s began, the group tried to promote grassroots involvement in its campaign to remove cartoons from theaters. Madison Jones advised Richard Riess to "get as many lay persons [as possible] to protest," adding, "We of course, always work on these matters, but when you get the consuming public to act sometimes a great deal more results from the protest." Still, the NAACP's shift toward focusing on television left no one available to act on a woman's complaint to the organization's New York branch about the "negroid facial and speech characteristics" in the "mammy type" bird and her children in Warner Brothers' 1952 reissue of the "Merrie Melodies" episode *The Early Worm Gets the Bird* (1940). She noted, "There was no humor no cleverness about the short—merely that vicious prejudice," and fruitlessly urged the organization to prevent the cartoon "from doing any more damage."[37]

By now, very little representation of blacks remained, though some cartoonists held on for a few more years. The final chapter shows how they weaned themselves away completely from African American expression.

SEVEN

United Productions
and the End of Animated
Black Representation

C HANGES IN AFRICAN AMERICAN IMAGERY in the animation industry corresponded to a period of change in race relations which the nation entered after World War II. As African Americans began serving in
integrated military units and playing on major-league baseball teams in
the late 1940s, some independent cartoon producers used their films to
promote racial integration throughout society. At the same time, segregation still persisted in many communities, and audiences still enjoyed
crude caricatures of blacks. Hollywood animators found ways to preserve
racial humor without attracting anti-stereotype activists.

A pamphlet deemed subversive by the federal government was an un-
likely source of inspiration for animators. When adapting literature to
animation, studios usually drew from fairy tales, although government
information had been used for military training cartoons like "Private
Snafu." In the late 1940s, however, the pamphlet "Races of Mankind" by
Ruth Benedict and Gene Weltfish, professors of anthropology at Columbia
University, provided unusual inspiration. The United Service Organization
(USO) had asked the scholars to write the pamphlet for U.S. soldiers fighting alongside indigenous people of color in such areas as the Philippines
and the Solomon Islands during World War II. Although the authors argued that wealth and education affected performance on intelligence tests,
the armed forces withdrew the pamphlet from distribution and banned
it from military libraries on the grounds that it appeared to describe
Northern blacks as more intelligent than Southern whites. The authors'
rebuttals that they had found the causes to be environmental instead of
racial fell on deaf ears. Although Benedict died in 1948, Weltfish had to

defend her research and her patriotism to Senator Joseph McCarthy's Internal Security Committee and soon thereafter lost her professorship at Columbia.[1]

Despite the controversial history of the pamphlet, the independent animation studio United Productions of America (UPA) decided to adapt the pamphlet as a documentary cartoon to serve as a tool for improving not only race relations but also the images of blacks in films. The United Auto Workers had commissioned UPA to produce a film that would help ease racial tension in recently desegregrated union branches in the South. In the resulting cartoon, *Brotherhood of Man* (1947), prejudiced American suburbanites of various racial groups learn about the stereotypes that prohibit them from living together harmoniously with their neighbors. The cartoon uses visual humor to show that brain size does not determine intelligence in a scene featuring a cross-eyed narrator who says, "The largest brain on record was that of an imbecile." The cartoon illustrates the pamphlet's argument that environment determines behavior in an amusing dialogue between a business-suited Chinese American who asks, "Got a match, bud?" while a white character in Chinese clothing answers him in Chinese.[2]

The radical look of the film visually complements the revolutionary racial theme. Each character in the film has the same facial design, in particular a pointed nose inspired, according to supervising director John Hubley, by the print cartoonist Saul Steinberg's drawings. The cartoon's black character thus broke with the standard racial image of large lips and bulging eyes. In addition, the backgrounds are very linear and spare in comparison to the usual heavily detailed scenes—a technique popularized by Disney in the 1930s.[3]

At the same time, *Brotherhood of Man* was itself participating in systemic racism by using racial stereotypes to illustrate cultural differences. For example, in the cartoon the neighbors do not all live in the same kind of home; an Eskimo's igloo and an African's hut appear next to the white man's house. To be sure, the film does not set out to stress the Americanness of different groups or the blending of the races into a "melting pot"; instead it promotes acceptance of and respect for cultural differences. Aside from the narrator, however, only the white man has a speaking role. Consequently, the film discusses multicultural sensitivity from the white point of view without taking into account the specific concerns of the other racial groups represented.

Nevertheless, the progressive graphics, humor, and racial message of *Brotherhood of Man* attracted attention in the press for months. Covering the sneak preview of the film at the New York Preview Theatre in May 1946, the *New York Times* called the film "a plea for racial tolerance . . . setting forth the theory that most differences today are a result of environment and bigotry." Never before had the newspaper heralded the developmental stage of an unreleased ten-minute cartoon short. Nor had the *Times* previously expressed such interest in the projects of an animation studio other than Disney's, especially a studio that lacked a major distributor. After the film's release in January 1947, writers in politically liberal magazines admired the integration of the message with pleasing graphics. Arthur Rosenheimer Jr. of *Theatre Arts* called the cartoon "a noble attempt to combat race prejudice through a witty and imaginative use of cartoon techniques." Philip T. Hartung of *Commonweal* lauded it as "a delight to watch," adding, "Even if you didn't believe in a single one of its ideas, you'd get pleasure out of its artistry and gay sense of humor. But chances are that you will be pleased with what this picture has to say." The critics' attention to the blending of cartoon artistry with civil rights advocacy attests to their surprise that animation and politics could coexist—and in such an entertaining fashion.[4]

The UPA film was in circulation at the same time as George Pal's *John Henry and the Inky-Poo,* with its groundbreaking black male hero, and both films simultaneously set new standards in animated black representation. In 1946 the *Hollywood Quarterly* lauded the racially progressive content of the two cartoons and lambasted the hoary caricatures prevalent in others. In contrast to the glowing reviews for Pal's "Puppetoons" series during World War II, film critic Sondra Gorney complained that cartoons starring the African American juvenile character Jasper "perpetuate the misconceptions of Negro characteristics." The critic Kenneth MacGowan suggested that *Brotherhood of Man* and *John Henry and the Inky-Poo* might pose serious threats to Disney's reign as animation's leading social commentator. As he put it: "They are significant because they show how the cartoon can comment on life and society and still be entertainment. Under present conditions such pioneering is probably not a thing for the feature-length cartoon to risk, but the short subject is another matter. Disney broke ground in the two-reelers which he made for the Office of Inter-American Affairs. He cannot wish to leave the field to his competitors."[5]

The "message movie" genre was the legacy that *Brotherhood of Man* left to Hollywood. This type of film, according to Ralph Ellison in *Shadow and Act*, deals not with African American issues but rather with white people's opinions of African Americans. Indeed, the cartoon directly addresses whites' assumptions about the inferior brain size, mental capabilities, and technological sophistication of people of color. Issues treated in later, feature-length message movies include the myth of the cowardly African American soldier in *Home of the Brave* (1949) and the biracial person's stereotypical tragic fate of having to chose between black and white identity in both *Lost Boundaries* (1949) and *Pinky* (1949). In this regard, these films reveal their roots in minstrelsy, for although minstrels' crude slapstick images of African Americans contrast with the message movies' upstanding black characters, both forms of entertainment are founded in whites' claims of accurately depicting blacks.[6]

UPA hoped to raise other social and political issues through animation, including "housing, atomic energy, international relations, juvenile delinquency and other post-war problems," according to the *New York Times*, but new commercial concerns thwarted those plans. In 1948 the studio abandoned public-interest documentaries for greater theatrical exposure when it arranged to produce apolitical slapstick cartoons such as episodes of "The Fox and the Crow" for distribution by Columbia Pictures. UPA later created "Mister Magoo"—the studio's longest-running series. The distributor had never released a racially progressive and allegedly subversive cartoon before signing UPA and was not about to start doing so.[7]

Columbia's preference for inoffensive fare reflected the reality that the idealism behind *Brotherhood of Man* had become a liability in Hollywood. In 1947 the House Un-American Activities Committee (HUAC) subpoenaed the cartoon's four screenwriters along with Weltfish and questioned them about their alleged communist ties. The journalist I. F. Stone of *The Nation* emerged as the media's staunchest defender of *Brotherhood of Man*'s ethnic images. "It is significant," Stone wrote, "that among those cited for contempt [by HUAC] are men who have written or produced those few movies which give the Negro a break and attack anti-Semitism." In the case of *Brotherhood of Man*, this entailed showing African Americans and whites being born in the same hospital, graduating from the same college, and marching in unison to work. Studio animator Bill Melendez recalled in an interview that the committee "saw fit to destroy UPA," adding, "UPA was too liberal for the times."[8]

"Races of Mankind" inspired plans for a second cartoon, this one by Alexander Klein, which would have provided an opportunity for the NAACP to enter the animation industry. In early 1946 he sent the civil rights organization a script for *United We Stand*, "a unified, integrated film correcting fallacious notions leading to race and other prejudice," according to Klein. His request that the organization sponsor the production of the cartoon would have been a proactive measure by the group, which at the time was merely conducting reactive campaigns, protesting films already released to theaters.

Lacking the narrative structure and humor of *Brotherhood of Man*, the script of *United We Stand* is a strange combination of morbidity and gimmickry. Klein planned to combine images of the worst kinds of racism with other images of America's most popular live-action and animated celebrities. The introduction of the script calls for visual "incidents and episodes of race and other minority prejudice which set the stage for the problem." This was to climax in a montage of various people bearing the superimposed epithets "'Just a lazy nigger'; 'A smart Jew'; 'A real Aryan of the beat type'; 'A fine Protestant'; 'That Dumb Bohunk'; 'Nothing but a dopey Polack'; 'Can't trust a Chinaman'; 'Watch out for those Russians' etc., etc." Toward the end, the script juxtaposes with this montage "symbolic diagrams of men hanging from Nazi gallows, indicating the clear connection between seemingly simple acts of prejudice and the monstrous crimes of Nazi racists." Klein felt that using "cartoonists and their famous comic strip characters, such as Joe Palooka, Superman, Terry and the Pirates, etc." would "help tell this story."[9]

United We Stand displays more boldness in its presentation of racial problems than *Brotherhood of Man*. Klein's script specifically discusses discrimination against African Americans. One scene depicts workplace segregation: "Several white men and a negro are in a line approaching a desk at which a man is calling off their names. Two white men in a row are called up and given jobs. The Negro's name is called and he is told there's nothing for him. As he leaves and closes the door, the next white man is called and with a wink, the man at the desk tells him he is hired." *Brotherhood of Man,* by contrast, never acknowledges the existence of systemic racism in the United States but instead focuses on racism's roots in the prejudices of individuals. The cartoon vaguely acknowledges institutional racism by calling for "equal opportunity for everyone from the very beginning . . . an equal start in life . . . equal chance for health and medical care . . . and a good education . . . an equal chance for a job."[10]

Basing the script for *United We Stand* on "Races of Mankind" left several people in addition to Klein vulnerable to accusations of communism by the federal government. Cartoonists Joe Shuster ("Superman"), Milton Caniff ("Terry and the Pirates"), Burne Hogarth ("Tarzan"), and Ham Fisher ("Joe Palooka") had expressed their willingness to contribute their talents and popular characters to the film. Their association with a project based on allegedly communist literature had the potential to taint their careers. Ironically, their characters were among the most patriotic comic strip figures of World War II.[11]

The NAACP, also claiming patriotic reasons, refused to finance *United We Stand.* For years it had distanced itself from the American Communist Party (ACP), considering communism harmful to the fight for social and political equality in a democratic country. The organization actively weeded out communist infiltrators from its branches and publicly declared its aversion to the ideology. The NAACP disagreed with the ACP's focus on class issues rather than racial ones and challenged the lack of black leadership in the party. The NAACP also had to be careful in its associations. The federal government already saw civil rights activists themselves as un-American, charging that by publicizing domestic racial discrimination, their campaigns provided ammunition to communists, who proceeded to challenge the United States on its failure to realize its promises of equality for all people. The earlier controversy surrounding "Races of Mankind" made Klein's project especially unattractive to the NAACP. He never turned his script into a film.[12]

Hollywood's animation studios refused to take up the mantle of tolerant black imagery in the wake of *Brotherhood of Man* and *United We Stand.* Such films were not only politically risky but also financial gambles for exhibitors, who wanted films featuring established characters or familiar plots, not revolutionary racial documentaries. Instead of creating new, more sensitive black figures, animators merely stylized older ones and watered down their personalities.

By the early 1950s African American characters had significantly smaller but no less broad roles in cartoons set in the South. Studios still found black representation important in establishing a cartoon's Southern scene. The designs for black characters remained exaggerated, and musical scores cartoons still made reference to minstrel songs romanticizing slavery whenever black figures appeared on the screen. Such images, however, usually took up no more than twenty seconds of a seven-minute film. For example, the Warner Brothers cartoon *Mississippi Hare* (1949) contains a few brief scenes of African American cotton-pickers who accidentally pick Bugs Bunny and throw him aboard a riverboat. The film, directed by Chuck Jones, does not show the workers' faces. It does, however, identify them as Southern African Americans by having them sing "Dixie" in stereotypical dialect. The studio transcribes the lyrics as "Way down South in the land ob cotton / Old times dat're not forgotten," and "In Dixie Land I'll take my stand / To lib and die in Dixie."[13]

Studios also developed new means for characters who were not African American to poke fun at black people. During a blackface gag in *Mississippi Hare*, a shuffling Bugs Bunny sings "Camptown Races" in its original "dialect" form: "Gawine ta run all night, / Gawine ta run all day, / Ah bet my money on a bob tail nag / Somebody bet on da bay." Although the scene is less than thirty seconds long, through the song, the dance, and the blackface appearance of Bugs's adversary, the cartoon manages to romanticize slavery, make yet another reference to minstrelsy, and degrade African Americans, all in that short amount of time.[14]

Four years later another "Bugs Bunny" episode provided a finale to African American antebellum imagery that showed how little the ethnic group's representation had changed over four decades. It attests as well to the lack of creativity that the industry's animators and directors—many of them in their second or third decade of theatrical cartooning—were beginning to evidence. Director Friz Freleng's *Southern Fried Rabbit* (1953) was the last theatrical cartoon to poke fun at enslaved African Americans. The cartoon treats the issue of the physically violent punishment of slaves by masters as a joke—not unlike *Dixie Days* (1930) from nearly a quarter century earlier—and offers comic renditions of minstrel songs, a tactic dating back to Max Fleischer's silent-era musical cartoons. Other examples of the film's use of Civil War stereotypes for humor include putting Bugs Bunny in disguise as Abraham Lincoln and a plantation mistress. In one scene Bugs even appears in blackface as a slave and sings "My Old Kentucky Home" in order to fool a confederate soldier while crossing into the South to eat carrots. After upsetting the officer by singing a song celebrating Northerners, the bunny kneels on the ground, begging the soldier, "Don't beat me, massa! Please don't beat me, massa! Don't whip this tired ol' body!"

Although black representation persisted in films set in the antebellum era, black figures did not appear in cartoons about modern postwar society. At MGM, for example, Tex Avery's satires on technology have all-white casts. Starting with *The House of Tomorrow* (1949), Avery developed a series of cartoons featuring brief gags about inventions that bring more harm than convenience to their white consumers. These films poke fun at the plethora of appliances and other goods that companies created and sold after the war. Advertisers pitched these household items to white suburbanites, considering them the most likely group of people to purchase the goods; after all, whites increasingly owned their own homes after World War II, and their spending on household items increased by 240 percent from 1945 to 1950. These cartoons have a parallel in literature and movies made before the 1950s, which often depict blacks as dim-witted rural characters unable to master mechanical contraptions and the complexity of urban life. For instance, the 1938 Warner Brothers cartoon *Jungle Jitters* features an African "native" who accidentally sucks his entire straw hut into a vacuum cleaner. In Avery's films, however, it is the devices that are faulty, not the people operating them. Middle-class white characters thus become the victims of the machines that promise them more leisurely, luxurious lives. In *The House of Tomorrow*, a woman correctly places ingredients into a pressure cooker, but the contraption still explodes and destroys the house.[15]

The growing influence of UPA on the animation industry after World War II served to hasten the disappearance of black characters from cartoons. The studio populated its films with white human figures drawn in a stylized, linear fashion in stories that reflected contemporary social attitudes. Its film *Gerald McBoing Boing* (1951)—the Academy Award winner for best cartoon short subject in 1951—especially exemplified this trend. Just as Americans, according to David Riesman's contemporary study *The Lonely Crowd*, defined themselves more with reference to the opinions of others than to their own views, Gerald struggles to gain acceptance from his playmates despite having sound effects for a voice. Conversely, in UPA's "Mister Magoo" series (1949–59), the star character stubbornly refuses to believe that his nearsightedness is causing him to violate social norms instead of conforming to them; in *Ragtime Bear* (1949), he mistakes a grizzly bear for his nephew and attempts to find lodging for it. Imitative films followed from competing studios, but they did not capture *Gerald McBoing Boing*'s charm or acclaim.[16]

By the early 1950s cartoon studios were adapting their animal and white human stars to the popular theme of white middle-class conformity while leaving black characters behind. Walt Disney, for example, completely transformed Goofy from a rural black-haired dog to a white "everyman" in a suit working at a downtown office. His skin was no longer jet black but pink, representing a white identity. Similarly, Warner Brothers' hunter figure Elmer Fudd was transformed into a white-collar worker. The changes created a similar effect to Harman-Ising's revamping of Bosko into a rural black boy; the characters became restricted to their suburban environments, just as Bosko had been banished to a Southern swamp. The few African American figures retained their traditional servile jobs—a reflection of the exclusion of the ethnic group from white-collar labor and middle-class suburban neighborhoods. Two postwar Famous Studios films—*Loose in the Caboose* (1947) and *Winter Draws On* (1948)—feature animated black train porters.[17]

Cartoon studios had discarded black characters in favor of blackface, one of the few types of African American representation that the NAACP and other groups did not protest. The blackface gags required little screen time; in a seven-minute cartoon, such a gag might appear for approximately five seconds. Also, characterization was minimal; few blackened characters spoke Negro dialect or wore the ragged clothes of Southern African American cartoon caricatures. Accordingly, blackface gags did not dominate cartoons, unlike NAACP targets such as the title character of Ub Iwerks's *Little Black Sambo* (1935) and the maid of MGM's *The Lonesome Mouse* (1943).

The violent blackface gag was one of many quick sight gags on which the postwar cartoon thrived. Studios continued to produce violent cartoons in the late 1940s and early 1950s, though the action was faster paced than in cartoons produced during the war. Series of cartoons built on chase sequences—ranging from "Tom and Jerry" to Warner Brothers' "Road Runner"—blended violence with speed. Other cartoons not constructed on chases tended to string together short sequences punctuated by swift and aggressive physical humor. Violent sight gags often incorporated weapons and explosives in order to keep up the pace of the chases and other quick-moving scenes. Bombs and firecrackers took only seconds to explode, instantly changing animal and white human characters into blackface caricatures.

Through the blackface gag, cartoons depict the image of the African American as the image of an "other." Cartoon characters do not retain their normal appearance after explosions and gunshots. They die, they have partially or completely charred bodies, or they turn into blackface caricatures. Because a character's blackened face represents an injured or damaged face, black features thus connote abnormality. The gag's humor comes from the suddenness of the abnormality, as shown in the dialogue continuity for MGM's cartoon *Daredevil Droopy* (1951): "The net tosses [Spike Bulldog] back up abreast of the platform just as the firecracker explodes, leaving Spike in comic black-face." This gag is one of many that leaves Spike physically distorted in the film; others include a gag in which Spike's body separates into cubes after falling through a net and another in which only his outline remains after he sets his own body on fire.[18]

The blackface gags of the postwar years show how few changes the studios had made in African American caricature since the 1910s. At a time when African Americans were seeking recognition of their civil and human rights, many cartoons still likened the ethnic group to animals. Although animators had developed more sophisticated designs for animal characters since the early years of sound films, characters such as Tom and Jerry still needed only to have their faces colored jet black and their mouths light brown or pink in order to become African American caricatures. Cartoon stories occasionally called for characters to mistake a blackfaced animal for an African American person. The script for the "Tom and Jerry" cartoon *Mouse Cleaning* (1948) provided guidelines for turning a blackened Tom Cat into an African American caricature convincing enough to fool the maid: "Tom, with a black face, pokes his head up thru the coal. . . . When she [the maid] questions him he answers in a broad colored dialect, 'No, mam. I ain't seen NO cat aroun' here.' He crawls out of the coal to his feet and continues talking, 'Un unh, ain't no cat, no place, no how—no mam.' He starts walking away in a shuffle with a wary expression but snaps into a horrified take as she yells, 'Thomas!! Come back here.'"[19]

The association of minstrel songs with blackface gags in cartoons helped to present the black image as an escapist "other" image. Musical scores from cartoons frequently contained portions of Stephen Foster tunes to accompany gags in which middle-class or upper-class characters were transformed into poor African American rural folk. Refusing to address African Americans' postwar concerns, the studios embraced the antebellum "benevolent master–loyal slave" stereotype in songs whose titles referred to slavery, allowing the blackface representations and musical associations to justify contemporary practices of segregation such as the de facto exclusion by whites of African Americans from suburban neighborhoods. The blackface "other" represents the incongruity of the "primitive" African American in an affluent white suburb. The films even depict the darkened characters as evil intruders in peaceful societies. MGM used the song "Massa's in the Cold Ground" in *The Flying Cat* (1952), in which Jerry sets fire to a ladder that Tom is using to reach a birdhouse in a suburban backyard. The blackened Tom is the unwelcome visitor to the bird's neighborhood.[20]

The scripts for MGM cartoons released between 1946 and 1953 reveal a systematic blackfacing. Studio directors Tex Avery and Dick Lundy followed the Hanna-Barbera team's lead in relying on gratuitous racial caricature for jokes. Several official studio documents refer to any character performing the explosion gags as "blackfaced." In describing the character's appearance, the scripts use such ethnic identifiers as "pickaninny," "mammy," and "darky," each of which carries a different set of connotations. Animators used the "pickaninny" blackface caricature to a character's immaturity as well as the inferiority of women, tying ethnicity together with gender in the process. After cartoon explosions, male figures are occasionally made to resemble caricatures of African American girls. To create this image, animators drew beribboned pigtails onto blackfaced characters. Tom and rival cat Butch appear this way after a gas oven explosion (courtesy of Jerry Mouse's match) in the Hanna-Barbera cartoon *A Mouse in the House* (1947). According to the script, "There is a terrific explosion, the cats swing from oven door, blinking at audience, looking like pickaninnies." In the script for the release *Life with Tom* (1953), Tom is seen "charred and looking like a pickaninny" after Jerry throws a lit candle that lands on the cat's tail. The same film's dialogue sheet calls for the fur on top of Tom's head to be burned to "stubs resembling small tufts of hair tied with ribbons."[21]

The blackfaced "mammy" in scripts is the most sexualized representation of African Americans in postwaranimation. The characters wear bandannas when blackfaced for the "mammy" look, but the scripts also give the "mammies" smaller co-stars to act as their children, although mammy characters in films—live action and animated—rarely have children of their own, especially on screen. The mammy characterization in blackface gags, while still stereotypical, nevertheless acknowledges the femininity of the characterization. The script for MGM's "Tom and Jerry" cartoon *The Little Orphan*, later released as *The Milky Waif* (1946), details the stereotypical construction of a mammy disguise:

(Scene 40) Jerry sees shoe polish and starts smearing it on face. . . .
(Scene 42) Pan of Jerry shuffling out from under door, dressed as Negro Mammy. He says, "How'd do Mist'r Tom. Hurry up Honey Child."
(Scene 43) Orphan waddles out from under door, dressed like a little pickaninny.

Similarly, in the script for Dick Lundy's cartoon *Little Wise Quacker* (1952), Barney Bear is seen "looking like a 'mammy'" when electrocuted while hunting a duck; his hunting cap serves as his bandanna. After the duck falls into Barney's arms, the bear proceeds to sing "Shortenin' Bread" to him while rocking him to sleep, according to the dialogue sheet.[22]

The script for Avery's cartoon *Droopy's Good Deed* (1951) uses the blackface gag to associate ethnicity with class. Rich, sophisticated white characters are transformed into poor, uneducated African American characters after a bomb explodes in front of them. The gag depicts the African Americans as the polarized opposite "other" to the whites, thus acknowledging that African Americans did not have the economic power and affluence of whites but making no reference to the reasons for the economic disparity between the two ethnic groups. Spike Bulldog plants a bomb in a top hat, which Droopy Dog proceeds to return to an elderly man. When Spike sees the money in the man's wallet, he shoves Droopy aside to collect the reward. After the explosion, according to the script, "we see the man and Spike as colored folk, the former still counting [the money] but in a darky dialect." This "darky dialect" also signifies mathematical ineptitude according to the film's dialogue sheet, in which the man counts, "Fifty-five, seventy, ninety-five, a hundred 'n' twenty, seventy-two, nine billion, frillion an' two bits."[23]

African American celebrity representation is a key part of many blackface gags. By associating the gags with well-known African American actors, including some who had not performed in years, the studios drew from Hollywood's African American history. In post–World War II cartoons animal and white characters with burnt faces speak in Eddie "Rochester" Anderson's gravelly voice, or they occasionally sport Stepin' Fetchit's slow, shuffling gait and half-closed eyes. By the late 1940s Anderson had been starring as Jack Benny's humble but clever servant for a decade. Warner Brothers, however, capitalized on his character's voice and ethnicity, not his cleverness, for blackface gags in *Bacall to Arms* (1946) and *I Taw a Putty Tat* (1948). Fetchit, meanwhile, had not starred in movies in almost a decade. Still, the script for the cartoon *Garden Gopher* (1950) has only to mention the actor's name in order to justify a blackfaced Spike Bulldog's slowness and shuffling: "The powder explodes and when the smoke clears we see a blackened dog walking a la Stepin' Fetchit."[24]

One of the last depictions of an African American jazz celebrity in Hollywood animation made a visual pun out of a jazz group via blackface. The script for the cartoon *Magical Maestro* (1952) associates a blackface gag with the name of the contemporary African American singing group the Ink Spots. The gag calls for a man to squirt ink from a pen into a baritone singer's face. Then, according to the script, "[two] tiny rabbits appear by his side in black-face and the trio sings a typical 'Ink Spot' selection—'Everything I Have Is Yours, You're Part of Me.'" After the same man drops an anvil on the baritone, he "becomes short and *talks* the song a la deep-voiced 'Ink Spot.'" Twenty years after Fleischer's *Minnie the Moocher* celebrated Cab Calloway's singing and dancing, contemporary African American music was still influencing cartoon humor, even if at the expense of the musicians. The scene nevertheless demonstrates Avery's familiarity with the group's performance style, and his direction as to how the baritone is to sing represents a significant improvement over the directive for the "coon-shouting" of a Calloway figure in Friz Freleng's *Clean Pastures* (1937).[25]

As UPA won Academy Awards for films that rejected cheap racial jokes, other studios eventually abandoned racial slapstick. The only cartoon that attempted to illustrate African Americans with UPA-inspired stylization was Walt Disney's *Toot, Whistle, Plunk, and Boom* (1953). To be sure, it demonstrated Disney's waning influence in American animation, for instead of creating a design for a minstrel character that other studios would later adopt, as Disney had done for the mammy, his studio presented a minstrel whose design revealed another studio's influence. Still, the result was a new type of African American image. One scene features two blackface minstrels plunking banjos. The characters sport the minstrels' traditional oversized collars and bowties but do not look like traditional minstrels. Their lips, though still big, are now angular instead of oval. The limited animation restricts movement to the minstrels' arms as they play their instruments. Disney's use of UPA-influenced stylization for minstrel figures ironically illustrates how divorced that technique had become by the mid-1950s from its roots in non-stereotypical black images in *Brotherhood of Man*.

Disney continued a long-standing practice of experimenting with technology in black representation. Just as he had used minstrel tunes to introduce animation to sound in *Steamboat Willie* in 1928, he now combined the century-old image of blackface with the new technology of CinemaScope in *Toot, Whistle, Plunk, and Boom*. CinemaScope was one of many visual gimmicks that both animation and live-action studios used to lure people away from the new medium of television and back into theaters. Movie attendance had begun dropping in 1946, not just because of competition from television, which was still rare, but also because of the movie industry's failure to adapt to audiences' changing tastes. Animating a character for a CinemaScope cartoon, however, required new techniques. Since the wide screen made artists' mistakes more obvious, animators had to use heavier lines of ink around each figure and cut back on character movement to reduce the visibility of errors. The blackface figures of *Toot, Whistle, Plunk, and Boom* were among the first to display heavier inking, which contributed to their angular design, as well as minimal movement.[26]

Toot, Whistle, Plunk, and Boom won the Academy Award in March 1954—an honor that signaled the beginning of the end of African American cartoon imagery. Unlike other award-winning films featuring black representation, this newest honoree inspired no new trends in black caricature. Competing studios did not begin designing black characters in similar UPA-inspired stylization. Even Hanna and Barbera for the first time in their directorial careers produced all of their cartoons for the entire year without including a single African American figure. Some animators experimented with UPA-like stories of white conformity; others stayed with their violent animal characters. The anti-stereotype movement had made black caricature risky for distributors, however, and the conformity stories spoke more to the times than did references to slaves and mammies.

Meanwhile, the director who had revolutionized American animation by first drawing from African American cultural expression retired from the industry. After moving from MGM to Walter Lantz's studio in 1953, Tex Avery left Lantz on August 20, 1954, and made no more theatrical cartoons. His departure created a void in animated black representation that no other director even dared to fill. Without a new inspiration like the bebop aesthetic and folktale references that Avery had introduced into the medium, Hollywood's remaining cartoonists fell into a creative rut. Cartoons increasingly fell back on violent animal chases (Sylvester Cat pursuing Tweety, Tom chasing Jerry), and studios developed new characters such as Warner's Speedy Gonzales to fit the chase formula.[27]

Animated black representation was ending where it had begun. The blackface image—dating back to 1907 with J. Stuart Blackton's "trick-films"—still appeared in cartoons but with decreasing frequency. Blackface, however, had a different context in 1954 than in the early 1900s. In the first half of the century, blackface was a necessity for studios producing cartoons on a rigorous schedule; the design enabled artists to animate characters without having to redraw intricate details with each movement. But by the 1950s, blackface had become an "other" image, no longer a character's normal appearance but rather an image so abnormal as to represent physical injury.

The December 1954 release of Famous Studios' last cartoon starring

Buzzy the Crow brought to a close over four decades of African American caricature in at least one short per year. In 1955, for the first time since 1912, no images of African Americans appeared in an entire year's worth of new animated theatrical shorts. The ethnic group's time in American animation had passed. Animators no longer used African American culture or white interpretations of it to construct films. In this they were merely following a current trend in American culture; in the 1950s the movies too shunned broad ethnic stereotypes, and television networks avoided programming construed as offensive to civil rights organizations.[28]

No theatrical cartoon studio created an alternative black image to the servile, crude, hyperactive clowns of the preceding half century. The cartoon directors of the 1950s, many with animation careers dating back to the 1920s, had no experience in developing such a figure. Even this failure also mirrors trends in other media. Television networks had already begun offering only programs starring all-white casts in the wake of the NAACP's protests of *Amos 'n' Andy* and *Beulah*. In addition, cartoon studios were losing money as television ate away at movie attendance. They could not afford the luxury of experimenting with new conceptions of African Americans. When black caricatures outlived their usefulness to the industry, they simply faded from the screen.

CONCLUSION

The Legacy of Animated African American Expression

As ANIMATION STUDIOS struggled to stay open over the next two decades, they tried to retain their formulas for caricaturing blacks without drawing black figures. Having served as the foundation of the theatrical cartoon industry for over fifty years, African American culture had become inextricable from animation. When Friz Freleng sought to modernize the fairy tale *Three Little Pigs* for a "Looney Tunes" episode, he cast the pink animals as bebop musicians, dressed them in zoot suits, gave them slang words to speak, and called the film *Three Little Bops* (1957). "Southern" animal characters of the 1960s such as Terrytoons' Deputy Dawg and Possible Possum inherited the "Negro dialect" once spoken by sambos, mammies, and other black characters.

Nevertheless, these revisions of African American expression failed to reverse the fortunes of theatrical animation. Having failed to attract new artists with fresh ideas, the studios found fewer exhibitors for their cartoons and finally closed their doors. The last of the holdouts were Walter Lantz Productions and Terrytoons, both of which shut down in 1972. African American representation, which had helped make possible the existence of American animation, had become the art form's albatross.[1]

Network television initially shunned cartoons starring black figures, not daring to risk the wrath of civil rights groups. To be sure, networks were willing to broadcast old theatrical cartoons, since few studios were producing cartoons for television in the 1950s. Walt Disney and Terrytoons reaped fortunes by licensing ABC and CBS to air their films (as *Disneyland* and *The Mighty Mouse Playhouse*, respectively). Walter Lantz also had success in packaging his films as *The Woody Woodpecker Show*, but ABC barred black figures from the series—a decision that ruled out the broadcasting of "Swing Symphonies" episodes, among other films.

Then, in the late 1960s, television animators found new ways to depict African Americans without using the old characterizations. By this time live-action television programs such as *Julia* and *Room 222* had appeared, featuring integrated casts of principal characters. Cartoon studios soon followed suit with television series such as *The Hardy Boys* and *Josie and the Pussycats*. Unlike the live-action shows, however, the cartoons did not mention race, nor did racial conflict figure in the plots. Nearly a quarter century after the House Un-American Activities Committee examined *Brotherhood of Man* for communist content, studios were still skittish about openly discussing racial equality. Integrated apolitical cartoons soon became standard fare not only on television but also in feature films. The trend continues in movies such as *The Incredibles*.

In the early 1970s studios gave urban black imagery a contemporary look when they began co-producing television cartoons in association with African Americans. Blacks now had unprecedented control over their own images on television; for example, the comedian Flip Wilson produced, wrote, and starred in material for his own variety series, which aired on NBC from 1970 to 1974. Capitalizing on this trend, the recording company Motown supervised production of the cartoon series based on the singing group the Jackson Five in 1971, and the following year comedian Bill Cosby not only oversaw but also starred in *Fat Albert and the Cosby Kids*. Both series featured modern rhythm-and-blues music scores, and the characters dressed in popular clothing styles of the day and often uttered slang words and phrases of the 1970s. Unlike the old cartoons starring zoot-suited musicians, the new cartoons did not poke fun at the culture. As with the integrated shows, these all-black animated programs avoided discussions of race, although such apolitical content was also consistent with the absence of social commentary from both Motown songs and the stand-up routines of Cosby.

The last frontier in animated black representation was black politics, which white animators had diluted in films beginning in World War II. While strong black political views had been featured in live-action comedy television shows such as *In Living Color* since the early 1990s, the animation industry was slow to adapt racial political humor to its medium. Then in 2005 Cartoon Network brought black cartoonist Aaron McGruder's comic strip "Boondocks" to animation. With McGruder controlling the content of the show, the series echoed the comic strip's liberal political rhetoric and discussions of social problems plaguing blacks.

Yet *Boondocks* also resurrected racial taboos in animation. Episodes of McGruder's series contained frequent utterances of the word "nigger" by multiple characters. To be sure, Walter Lantz Productions and other old studios had used the slur to describe characters in scripts, but no cartoon figures had spoken it in films since the 1930s. The NAACP had called a Hollywood studio executive to task for using the word during the *Scrub Me Mama with a Boogie Beat* campaign of 1948–49. But now it was being used in a different context, not in a cartoon by a white artist depicting blacks as big-lipped, lazy farm laborers, but in a series by a black cartoonist about urban, modern blacks.

As for the old cartoons released between the early 1900s and the 1950s, their legacy is mixed. None of the films air on network television without heavy censorship. For example, Cartoon Network dubbed a new actor speaking grammatically correct lines for the "Tom and Jerry" maid over Lillian Randolph's original "Negro dialect." Still, film purists regret such tampering. Whatever views people may have about black representation in theatrical films, the depictions stand as primary examples of black imagery in popular culture from the era of lynchings to the birth of the civil rights movement.

NOTES

Introduction

1. Eric Lott, *Love and Theft: Blackface Minstrelsy and the American Working Class* (New York: Oxford University Press, 1995), 3–12.

1. The Silent Era

1. Donald Crafton, *Before Mickey* (Cambridge: MIT Press, 1982), 9, 57.
2. Ibid., 110; Leslie Cabarga, *The Fleischer Story* (New York: Da Capo Press, 1988), 18.
3. Cabarga, *The Fleischer Story,* 16.
4. Crafton, *Before Mickey,* 153.
5. Cabarga, *The Fleischer Story,* 17.
6. John Higham, *Strangers in the Land* (New Brunswick, N.J.: Rutgers University Press, 1955), 196–97, 242, 264–65.
7. Jack Zander to author, April 18, 2000; Shamus Culhane, *Talking Animals and Other People* (New York: St. Martin's Press, 1986), 41–42.
8. Zander to author, April 18, 2000.
9. Elizabeth Hay, *Sambo Sahib* (Totowa, N.J.: Barnes & Noble, 1981), 156; Phyllis J. Yuill, *Little Black Sambo: A Closer Look* (New York: Racism and Sexism Resource Center for Educators, 1976), 3.
10. Fredrik Stromberg, *Black Images in the Comics* (Seoul: Fantagraphics, 2003), 55.
11. Crafton, *Before Mickey,* 149, 169, 175; Cabarga, *The Fleischer Story,* 18.
12. Crafton, *Before Mickey,* 287; Creighton Peet, "The Cartoon Comedy," *New Republic,* August 14, 1929, 342.
13. Leonard Maltin, *Of Mice and Magic: A History of American Animated Cartoons* (New York: Plume, 1987), 129.
14. Crafton, *Before Mickey,* 310; Maltin, *Of Mice and Magic,* 201.
15. *Dinner Time*—the first sound cartoon, produced by Amadee Van Beuren—had preceded Mickey's first appearance in theaters by two months but caused no stir because of its failure to blend visual humor effectively with sound.

2. The Arrival of Sound

1. Scott Curtis, "The Sound of the Early Warner Bros. Cartoons," in *Sound Theory, Sound Practice,* ed. Rick Altman (New York: Routledge, 1992), 195–97; "Looney Tunes," advertisement, *Variety,* June 25, 1930, 73.
2. Jack Zander to author, April 18, 2000.
3. "Talking Shorts: *Box Car Blues,*" *Variety,* March 11, 1931, 14. Mel Shaw relates Bosko to Felix in Charles Solomon's book *Enchanted Drawings* (New York: Alfred A. Knopf, 1989), 100. "Talking Shorts: *Congo Jazz,*" *Variety,* August 20, 1930, 14; Zander to author, February 9, 1999. Zander's story also appears in Leonard Maltin, *Of Mice and Magic: A History of American Animated Cartoons* (New York: Plume, 1987), 225.

4. Thomas Cripps, *Slow Fade to Black: The Negro in American Film, 1900–1942* (Oxford: Oxford University Press, 1993), 236–40.

5. Leslie A. Fiedler, *The Inadvertent Epic: From Uncle Tom's Cabin to Roots* (New York: Simon and Schuster, 1979), 26–27, 48; Harriet Beecher Stowe, *Uncle Tom's Cabin* (1852; reprint, New York: Signet Classic, 1966), 417.

6. W. C. Handy, "St. Louis Blues," in *Call and Response: The Riverside Anthology of the African American Literary Tradition*, ed. Patricia Liggins Hill (Boston: Houghton Mifflin, 1998), 572.

7. "Talking Shorts: *Dixie Days*," *Variety*, May 21, 1930, 19; "180 Days for Aesop Fable," *Exhibitors' Herald-World*, April 26, 1930, 45. *Exhibitors' Herald-World* became *Motion Picture Herald* in the mid-1930s.

8. Henry T. Sampson, *That's Enough, Folks: Black Images in Animated Cartoons, 1900–1960* (Lanham, Md.: Scarecrow Press, 1998), 139, 142.

9. Shamus Culhane, *Talking Animals and Other People* (New York: St. Martin's Press, 1986), 53.

10. Leslie Cabarga, *The Fleischer Story* (New York: Da Capo Press, 1988), 50–51; Cheryl Lynn Greenberg, *Or Does It Explode? Black Harlem in the Great Depression* (New York: Oxford University Press, 1991), 177.

11. Culhane, *Talking Animals and Other People*, 43.

12. Myron Waldman to author, July 25, 1997.

13. Culhane, *Talking Animals and Other People*, 52; "Talking Shorts: *Hot Dog*," *Variety*, April 16, 1930, 21; "Talking Shorts: *Ace of Spades*," *Variety*, March 25, 1931, 16.

14. "Talking Shorts: *Blues*," *Variety*, June 30, 1931, 15.

15. "Talking Shorts: *Cuckoo Murder Case*," *Variety*, October 29, 1930, 17; Gilbert Seldes, "Disney and Others," *New Republic*, June 8, 1932, 101.

16. "Talking Shorts: *Plane Dumb*," *Variety*, November 22, 1932, 16; Robert Sklar, *Movie-Made America: A Cultural History of American Movies*, rev. and updated ed. (New York: Vintage Books, 1994), 16, 58; Eric Lott, *Love and Theft: Blackface Minstrelsy and the American Working Class* (New York: Oxford University Press, 1993), 96, 156.

17. Melvin Patrick Ely, *The Adventures of Amos 'n' Andy: A Social History of an American Phenomenon* (New York: Free Press, 1990), 29; David Levering Lewis, *When Harlem Was in Vogue* (New York: Oxford University Press, 1989), 211.

18. *The Rasslin' Match*, advertisement, *Variety*, January 9, 1934, 13; Bill Littlejohn, telephone interview with author, January 19, 1999.

19. Cripps, *Slow Fade to Black*, 269–70.

20. *The Rasslin' Match*, advertisement; J. J. Medford, "What the Picture Did for Me: *The Rasslin' Match*," *Motion Picture Herald*, June 23, 1934, 137; A. N. Miles, "What the Picture Did for Me: *The Rasslin' Match*," *Motion Picture Herald*, April 7, 1934, 84.

21. Littlejohn, telephone interviewed, January 11, 1999.

22. Ibid.; Siegfried Kracauer, *Theory of Film: The Redemption of Physical Reality* (New York: Oxford University Press, 1960), 100.

23. Waldman to author, July 25, 1997.

24. Cabarga, *The Fleischer Story*, 63.

25. Norman M. Klein, *7 Minutes: The Life and Death of the American Animated Cartoon* (London: Verso, 1993), 62.

26. Lott, *Love and Theft*, 41; Cabarga, *Fleischer Story*, 63; Kracauer, *Theory of Film*, 100; J. J. Medford, "What the Picture Did for Me: *I'll Be Glad When You're Dead You Rascal You*," *Motion Picture Herald*, October 7, 1933, 56.

27. Lewis, *When Harlem Was in Vogue*, 240, 242.

28. Klein, *7 Minutes*, 70–71.

29. Paul Wells, *Understanding Animation* (London: Routledge, 1998), 217.

30. Jake Austen, "Hidey Hidey Hidey Ho . . . Boop-Boop-A-Doop! The Fleischer Studio and

Jazz Cartoons," in *The Cartoon Music Book*, ed. Daniel Goldmark and Yuval Taylor (Chicago: A Cappella Books, 2002), 65–66.

31. Culhane, *Talking Animals and Other People*, 47; Berny Wolf to author, February 1998; Cabarga, *Fleischer Story*, 63.

32. Henry Reeve, "What the Picture Did for Me: *The Old Man of the Mountains*," *Variety*, October 21, 1933, 53.

33. Thomas Doherty, *Pre-Code Hollywood: Sex, Immorality, and Insurrection in American Cinema, 1930–1934* (New York: Columbia University Press, 1999), 325; Cabarga, *Fleischer Story*, 81.

34. Myron Waldman to author, March 9, 1999; Lewis, *When Harlem Was in Vogue*, 306.

3. Black Characterizations

1. Leonard Leff, *Dame in the Kimono: Hollywood, Censorship, and the Production Code*, 2nd ed. (Lexington: University Press of Kentucky, 2001), 288–89, 300.

2. Ibid., 28–29.

3. Robert Sklar, *Movie-Made America: A Cultural History of American Movies* (New York: Vintage Books, 1994), 187, 194.

4. Mel Shaw, quoted in Charles Solomon, *Enchanted Drawings* (New York: Alfred A. Knopf, 1989), 145; *Swing Wedding*, dialogue continuity, Metro-Goldwyn-Mayer Collection, University of Southern California Archives, 1.

5. *The Old Millpond*, dialogue continuity, May 20, 1936, Metro-Goldwyn-Mayer Collection, University of Southern California Archives, 2, 4, 8.

6. Ibid., 3, 7; *Swing Wedding*, 6.

7. *Swing Wedding*, 2, 7.

8. *Clean Pastures*, transcription, Warner Brothers Archives, University of Southern California, 1, 2. According to Schlesinger director Chuck Jones, in *Chuck Amuck: The Life and Times of an Animated Cartoonist* (New York: Farrar Straus Giroux, 1989), 154, 172, a director had the final say as to the content of scripts.

9. Karl Cohen, *Forbidden Animation: Censored Cartoons and Blacklisted Animators in America* (Jefferson, N.C.: McFarland & Co., 1997), 29; Michael Barrier, *Hollywood Cartoons: American Animation in Its Golden Age* (New York: Oxford University Press, 1999), 342.

10. Motion Picture Producers and Distributors Association Board of Directors, Minutes of meeting, October 25, 1937; *Clean Pastures* file, Warner Brothers Archives, University of Southern California; Joseph Breen to Leon Schlesinger, May 11, 1937, *Clean Pastures* file.

11. H. M. Warner to Will Hays, May 25, 1937, *Clean Pastures* file, Warner Brothers Archives, University of Southern California.

12. Ibid.

13. Joseph Breen to Leon Schelsinger, November 5, 1937, and Will Hays and Joseph Breen to Harry Warner, October 12, 1937, both *Clean Pastures* file, Warner Brothers Archives, University of Southern California.

14. *Clean Pastures*, 3. For the rapture, see 1 Thessalonians 4:17.

15. *The Goose Goes South*, script, 1940, Metro-Goldwyn-Mayer Collection, University of Southern California Archives, 6.

16. Henry T. Sampson, *That's Enough, Folks: Black Images in Animated Cartoons, 1900–1960* (Lanham, Md.: Scarecrow Press, 1998), 148; Sterling Brown, *The Negro in American Fiction* (New York: Atheneum, 1972), 106.

17. Edward D. C. Campbell Jr., *Celluloid South: Hollywood and the Southern Myth* (Knoxville: University of Tennessee Press, 1981), 74–75.

18. Eugene D. Genovese, *Roll, Jordan, Roll: The World the Slaves Made* (New York: Pantheon, 1974), 4–6.

19. *The Old Plantation*, dialogue continuity, Metro-Goldwyn-Mayer Collection, University of Southern California Archives, 2–3, 7.

20. *Swing Social*, script, 1940, Metro-Goldwyn-Mayer Collection, University of Southern California Archives, 4–5.

21. Joseph Barbera, *My Life in 'Toons: From Flatbush to Bedrock in Under a Century* (Atlanta: Turner Publishing, 1994), 76; "*Swing Social*," 3.

22. *Scrub Me Mama with a Boogie Beat*, synopsis, Walter Lantz Animation Archive, collection number 47, UCLA Arts Library Special Collections.

23. *The Goose Goes South*, 5.

24. *The Old Plantation*, 2, 7.

25. *The Bookworm*, script, 1939, Metro-Goldwyn-Mayer Collection, University of Southern California Archives, 7.

26. *Fraidy Cat*, script, 1942, Metro-Goldwyn-Mayer Collection, University of Southern California Archives, 10.

27. Stefan Kanfer, *Serious Business: The Art and Commerce of Animation in America from Betty Boop to Toy Story* (New York: Scribner, 1997), 153; Leonard Maltin, *Of Mice and Magic: A History of American Animated Cartoons* (New York: Plume, 1987), 192, 293; *The Lonesome Mouse*, 6.

28. *Handle with Care*, script, 1940, Metro-Goldwyn-Mayer Collection, University of Southern California Archives, 3; *The Lonesome Mouse*, script, 1943, Metro-Goldwyn-Mayer Collection, University of Southern California Archives, 8; Jack Zander to author, February 9, 1999.

29. Zander to author, February 9, 1999.

30. Jacqueline Jones, *Labor of Love, Labor of Sorrow: Black Women, Work, and the Family from Slavery to the Present* (New York: Vintage Books, 1995), 237–39; Angela Y. Davis, *Blues Legacies and Black Feminism: Gertrude "Ma" Rainey, Bessie Smith, and Billie Holiday* (New York: Pantheon Books, 1998), 143, 349.

31. Mel Shaw quoted in Solomon, *Enchanted Drawings*, 100, 108.

32. L. A. Irwin, "What the Picture Did for Me: *Bosko and the Cannibals*," *Motion Picture Herald*, December 11, 1937, 71; A. J. Inks, "What the Picture Did for Me: *Bosko and the Cannibals*," *Motion Picture Herald*, December 4, 1937, 67

33. *The Old House*, dialogue continuity, August 13, 1936, Metro-Goldwyn-Mayer Collection, University of Southern California Archives, 2.

34. Maltin, *Of Mice and Magic*, 282; Irwin, 71; Inks, 67; "*Bosko and the Cannibals*," advertisement, *Atlanta Constitution*, 6 February 1938, 7b.

35. Brown, *Negro in American Fiction*, 106.

36. A. J. Inks, "What the Picture Did for Me: *Silly Superstition*," *Motion Picture Herald*, February 17, 1940, 50; Inks, "What the Picture Did for Me: *A Haunting We Will Go*," *Motion Picture Herald*, May 11, 1940, 64.

37. Sondra Gorney, "The Puppet and the Moppet," *Hollywood Quarterly* (July 1946): 372.

38. "Cinema: *Jasper and the Watermelons*," *Time*, March 9, 1942, 82–83.

39. Besa Short, "*Flop Goes the Weasel*," *Besa Short's Shorts*, March 30, 1943, 4.

40. Katharine Lewis, transcription of *Angel Puss*, Warner Brothers Archives, University of Southern California.

4. Fred "Tex" Avery and "Trickster" Animation

1. "*Uncle Tom's Bungalow*," transcription, Warner Brothers Archives, University of Southern California, 1–2.

2. Joel Dinerstein, "Lester Young and the Birth of Cool," in *Signifyin(g), Sanctifyin', and Slam Dunkin': A Reader in African American Expressive Culture*, ed. Gena Dagel Caponi (Amherst: University of Massachusetts Press, 1999), 250, 260; Ralph Ellison, *Shadow and Act* (New York: Random House, 1964), 211.

3. Ellison, *Shadow and Act*, 225; Joe Adamson, *Bugs Bunny: Fifty Years and Only One Grey Hare* (New York: A Donald Hutter Book, 1990), 54.

4. Joel Chandler Harris, *Uncle Remus: His Songs and His Sayings* (New York: Grosset and Dunlap, 1920), 54–63, 73–76.

5. Dinerstein, "Lester Young and the Birth of Cool," 253–54, 263–64.

6. Adamson, *Bugs Bunny*, 54.

7. Harris, *Uncle Remus*, 87–93.

8. Adamson, *Bugs Bunny*, 43.

9. Leonard Maltin, *Of Mice and Magic: A History of American Animated Cartoons* (New York: Plume, 1987), 51, 71; Shamus Culhane, *Talking Animals and Other People* (New York: St. Martin's Press, 1986), 239.

10. Robert Toll, *Blacking Up: The Minstrel Show in Nineteenth-Century America* (New York: Oxford University Press, 1974), 120, 121, 124; Ellison, *Shadow and Act*, 225.

11. Ellison, *Shadow and Act*, 212, 225; Adamson, *Bugs Bunny*, 58; Joe Adamson, *Tex Avery: King of Cartoons* (New York: Da Capo, 1975), 162.

12. Adamson, *Bugs Bunny*, 12.

13. Harris, *Uncle Remus*, 41–47; Michael Barrier, *Hollywood Cartoons: American Animation in Its Golden Age* (New York: Oxford University Press, 1999), 458–59.

14. Adamson, *Tex Avery*, 188.

15. Adamson, *Bugs Bunny*, 67.

5. Black Representation and World War II Political Concerns

1. "Schlesinger Artmen Finish Bond Briefie," *Hollywood Reporter*, December 16, 1941; Michael Rogin, *Blackface, White Noise: Jewish Immigrants in the Hollywood Melting Pot* (Berkeley: University of California Press, 1996), 167.

2. Martha Sigall, telephone interview with the author, February 13, 1998.

3. Walter White, *A Rising Wind* (Garden City, N.Y.: Doubleday, Doran and Co., 1945), 143; Nat Brandt, *Harlem at War: The Black Experience in World War II* (Syracuse University Press, 1996), 140, 227.

4. Pfc. Bruce O. Bishop, review of *Sunday Go to Meetin' Time*, *Pittsburgh Courier*, March 16, 1945, reprinted in Henry T. Sampson, *That's Enough, Folks: Black Images in Animated Cartoons, 1900–1960* (Lanham, Md.: Scarecrow Press, 1998), 209–10.

5. Brandt, *Harlem at War*, 111.

6. *Boogie Woogie Bugle Boy of Company B*, storyboard, Walter Lantz Animation Archive, collection number 47, UCLA Arts Library Special Collections; Arthur K. Dame, "What the Picture Did for Me: *Old Blackout Joe*," *Motion Picture Herald*, November 7, 1942, 45.

7. Katharine Lewis, transcription of *Coal Black an de Sebben Dwarfs*, 1942, Warner Brothers Archives, University of Southern California, 2; Thomas di Lorenzo, "What the Picture Did for Me: *Coal Black an de Sebben Dwarfs*," *Motion Picture Herald*, October 23, 1943, 53.

8. Norman M. Klein, *7 Minutes: The Life and Death of the American Animated Cartoon* (London: Verso, 1993), 131, 192–93.

9. Jerry Beck and Will Friedwald, *Looney Tunes and Merrie Melodies: A Complete Illustrated Guide to the Warner Bros. Cartoons* (New York: Owl, 1989), 137; Michael Barrier, *Hollywood Cartoons: American Animation in Its Golden Age* (New York: Oxford University Press, 1999), 440.

10. Leonard Maltin, *Of Mice and Magic: A History of American Animated Cartoons* (New York: Plume, 1987), 235; Bill Milkowski, *Swing It! An Annotated History of Jive* (New York: Billboard Books, 2001), 73; *Coal Black an de Sebben Dwarfs*, 1.

11. "Short Subject Release Sheet: *Coal Black an de Sebben Dwarfs*," 1943, Motion Picture, Broadcasting, and Recorded Sound Division, Library of Congress, Washington, D.C.; John W.

Dower, *War without Mercy: Race and Power in the Pacific War* (New York: Pantheon Books, 1986), 175.

12. Julia Baxter, "Memorandum to Miss Harper," April 16, 1943, Papers of the National Association for the Advancement of Colored People, Library of Congress, Washington, D.C.; Odette Harper, "Memorandum to Mr. White," April 9, 1943, ibid.; Walter White to Harry M. Warner, April 28, 1943, ibid.

13. Odette Harper, "Memorandum to Mr. White," April 17, 1943, ibid.; Lawrence R. Samuel, *Pledging Allegiance: American Identity and the Bond Drive of World War II* (Washington: Smithsonian Institute Press, 1997), 131; White, *A Rising Wind*, 147–48.

14. Thomas Cripps, *Making Movies Black: The Hollywood Message Movie from World War II to the Civil Rights Era* (New York: Oxford University Press, 1993), 197; Baxter, "Memorandum to Miss Harper."

15. Dower, *War without Mercy*, 175; *Boogie Woogie Bugle Boy of Company B*, script, Walter Lantz Animation Archive, collection number 47, UCLA Arts Library Special Collections; "*Yankee Doodle Swing Shift*," *Variety*, August 19, 1942, 21.

16. Shamus Culhane, *Talking Animals and Other People* (New York: St. Martin's Press, 1986), 252–53.

17. Milkowski, *Swing It!*, 36.

18. H. Goldson, "What the Picture Did for Me: *Goldilocks and the Jivin' Bears*," *Motion Picture Herald*, November 25, 1944, 50; Leona Sands, transcription of *Goldilocks and the Jivin' Bears*, 1944, Warner Brothers Archives, University of Southern California, 1.

19. Thomas di Lorenzo, "What the Picture Did for Me: *Eliza on the Ice*," *Motion Picture Herald*, October 7, 1944, 49.

20. Joseph Barbera, *My Life in 'Toons: From Flatbush to Bedrock in Under a Century* (Atlanta: Turner Publishing, 1994), 76.

21. *The Zoot Cat*, script, 1944, Metro-Goldwyn-Mayer Collection, University of Southern California Archives, 1.

22. Ibid., 5; Milkowski, *Swing It!*, 37; *Swing Social*, 4.

23. Herman Hill, "Film City Cartoonists Act to Correct Race Caricatures," *Pittsburgh Courier*, October 7, 1944, 13.

24. Ibid.

25. Ibid.

26. "Duke Ellington to Play in Puppetoon," *Pittsburgh Courier*, August 24, 1946, 18.

6. African American Representation and Changing Race Relations

1. "Little Jasper Series Draws Protest from Negro Groups," *Ebony* (January 1947): 30–31.

2. Sondra Gorney, "The Puppet and the Moppet," *Hollywood Quarterly* (July 1946): 372.

3. Brett Williams, *John Henry: A Bio-Bibliography* (Westport, Conn.: Greenwood, 1983), 17, 47.

4. Ibid., 84–141; Mel Watkins, *On the Real Side* (New York: Simon and Schuster, 1994), 271; "Little Jasper Series Draws Protest from Negro Groups," *Ebony* (January 1947): 30.

5. Madison Jones to Jack Strauss, June 9, 1949, Papers of the National Association for the Advancement of Colored People, Library of Congress, Washington, D.C.; H. Norman Neubert to Madison Jones, June 27, 1949, ibid.

6. Madison Jones to Castle Films, Inc., June 3, 1949, ibid.; M. Goodman to Madison Jones, July 27, 1949, ibid.

7. Charles M. Payne, *I've Got the Light of Freedom: The Organizing Tradition and the Mississippi Freedom Struggle* (Berkeley: University of California Press, 1995), 24–25.

8. Edward D. C. Campbell Jr., *The Celluloid South: Hollywood and the Southern Myth* (Knoxville: University of Tennessee Press, 1981), 146; *Uncle Tom's Cabana*, script, Metro-

Goldwyn-Mayer Collection, University of Southern California Archives, 1.

9. *Uncle Tom's Cabana*, 2; Leslie A. Fiedler, *The Inadvertent Epic: From Uncle Tom's Cabin to Roots* (New York: Touchstone, 1979), 48.

10. *Uncle Tom's Cabana*, 4; Arthur K. Dame, "What the Picture Did for Me: *Old Blackout Joe*," *Motion Picture Herald*, November 7, 1942, 45.

11. Edna Kerin, "Memorandum to Mr. Henry Moon," October 11, 1948, Papers of the National Association for the Advancement of Colored People, Library of Congress; Julia Baxter, "Memorandum to Mr. Henry Moon," October 11, 1948, ibid.

12. Thomas Cripps, *Making Movies Black: The Hollywood Message Movie from World War II to the Civil Rights Era* (New York: Oxford University Press, 1993), 48–49; Madison Jones, memorandum, November 4, 1948, Papers of the National Association for the Advancement of Colored People, Library of Congress, 3; E. L. McEvoy, letter to the NAACP, October 29, 1948, Papers of the National Association for the Advancement of Colored People, Library of Congress.

13. Jones, memorandum, 3.

14. Madison Jones to Emanuel Muravchik, December 28, 1948, Papers of the National Association for the Advancement of Colored People, Library of Congress; Irving Salert to Madison Jones, January 3, 1949, ibid.; Madison Jones, "Memorandum to Mr. White," February 18, 1949, ibid.

15. Emanuel Muravchik, telephone interview with author, April 18, 2001.

16. Elaine Tyler May, *Homeward Bound: American Families in the Cold War Era* (New York: Basic Books, 1982), 166; Jacqueline Jones, *Labor of Love, Labor of Sorrow: Black Women, Work, and the Family from Slavery to the Present* (New York: Vintage Books, 1995), 256.

17. *Old Rockin' Chair Tom*, script, January 8, 1947, Metro-Goldwyn-Mayer Collection, University of Southern California Archives, 5.

18. *Saturday Evening Puss*, dialogue sheet, March 29, 1948, ibid., 1; *A Mouse in the House*, script, ibid., 1.

19. *The Framed Cat*, script, December 16, 1948, ibid., 1; *Handle with Care*, 3; *Part Time Pal*, script, July 17, 1946, ibid., 1.

20. *Sittin' Kitten*, dialogue sheet, ibid., 1–2; *Cat of Tomorrow*, script, October 9, 1950, ibid., 1–2.

21. *Old Rockin' Chair Tom*, 10; *Old Rockin' Chair Tom*, dialogue sheet, ibid., 1.

22. *Part Time Pal*, 4–5; *Cat of Tomorrow*, 1.

23. *Cat of Tomorrow*, 6; Jones, *Labor of Love, Labor of Sorrow*, 256.

24. *Part Time Pal*, 5; *A Mouse in the House*, 5; *The Lonesome Mouse*, 4; *Old Rockin' Chair Tom*, script, 9.

25. *Old Rockin' Chair Tom*, dialogue sheet, 1; *Polka Dot Puss*, script, Metro-Goldwyn-Mayer Collection, University of Southern California Archives, 1.

26. Lillian Randolph quoted in Billy Rowe, "Facts Brought Out to Show That One Colored Artist Put Damper on AFRA Move," *Pittsburgh Courier*, October 11, 1947, 19; Franklin H. Williams, "Memorandum to Mr. Walter White," August 5, 1947, Papers of the National Association for the Advancement of Colored People, Library of Congress.

27. Richard O. Riess to Walter White, July 10, 1950, Papers of the National Association for the Advancement of Colored People, Library of Congress; Fred G. Weppler, "What the Picture Did for Me: *The Lonesome Mouse*," *Motion Picture Herald*, March 25, 1950, 42.

28. Ray McFarlane, "What the Picture Did for Me: *Push-Button Kitty*," *Motion Picture Herald*, May 16, 1953, 35; Madison Jones to Richard Riess, July 17, 1950, Papers of the National Association for the Advancement of Colored People, Library of Congress.

29. Edna Kerin, "Memorandum to Mr. White," October 31, 1949, Papers of the National Association for the Advancement of Colored People, Library of Congress; Robert H. Zieger, *The CIO, 1935–1955* (Chapel Hill: University of North Carolina Press, 1995), 254, 256, 290; Karl

Korstad, "Black and White Together," in *The CIO's Left-Led Unions*, ed. Steve Rosswurm (New Brunswick, N.J.: Rutgers University Press, 1992), 2.

30. On July 12, 1951, the *Hollywood Reporter*, 3, announced in the article "MGM Cartoon Slate Ready for Full Year" that all of MGM's cartoons for the 1951–52 season—*Push-Button Kitty* among them—were ready for booking on September 1. If the studio already had a completed Technicolor print of the mammy's final appearance, Randolph must have concluded her work on that cartoon as she was beginning work on *Amos 'n' Andy*, which first aired on CBS in January 1951.

31. Bill Milkowski, *Swing It! An Annotated History of Jive* (New York: Billboard Books, 2001), 105; John D. Ford, "An Interview with John and Faith Hubley," in *The American Animated Cartoon*, ed. Gerald Peary and Danny Peary (New York: Dutton, 1980), 187.

32. *Solid Serenade*, story synopsis, Metro-Goldwyn-Mayer Collection, University of Southern California Archives.

33. Milkowski, *Swing It!*, 105; Nat Brandt, *Harlem at War: The Black Experience in World War II* (Syracuse University Press, 1996), 227.

34. Watkins, *On the Real Side*, 289.

35. Roger D. Abrahams, *Afro-American Folktales: Stories from Black Traditions in the New World* (New York: Pantheon Books, 1985), 20; Leonard Maltin, *Of Mice and Magic: A History of American Animated Cartoons* (New York: Plume, 1987), 315.

36. Jackson Beck, telephone interview with author, February 5, 1998; Syd Raymond, telephone interview with author, September 11, 2002.

37. Jones to Riess, July 17, 1950; Helen Lapcheck to the NAACP, February 14, 1953, Papers of the National Association for the Advancement of Colored People, Library of Congress.

7. United Productions and the End of Animated Black Representation

1. Ruth E. Pathe, "Gene Weltfish, 1902–1980," in *Women Anthropologists: A Biographical Dictionary*, ed. Ute Gacs et al. (New York: Greenwood, 1988), 375–77; Judith Modell, "Ruth Fulton Benedict, 1887–1948," ibid., 5.

2. Ring Lardner Jr. et al., "Brotherhood of Man: A Script," *Hollywood Quarterly* (July 1946): 353, 358.

3. Michael Barrier, *Hollywood Cartoons: American Animation in Its Golden Age* (New York: Oxford University Press, 1999), 515, 527; John D. Ford, "An Interview with John and Faith Hubley," in *The American Animated Cartoon*, ed. Gerald Peary and Danny Peary (New York: Dutton, 1980), 185.

4. "Auto Workers Offer Film on Tolerance," *New York Times*, May 23, 1946, 16; Arthur Rosenheimer Jr., "Off the Main Stem," *Theatre Arts* (February 1947): 6–7; Philip T. Hartung, "It's Good for You," *Commonweal*, February 14, 1947, 446.

5. Sondra Gorney, "The Puppet and the Moppet,"*Hollywood Quarterly* (July 1946): 372; Kenneth MacGowan, "Make Mine Disney: A Review," ibid., 377.

6. Ralph Ellison, *Shadow and Act* (New York: Random House, 1964), 277; Michael Rogin, *Blackface, White Noise: Jewish Immigrants in the Hollywood Melting Pot* (Berkeley: University of California Press, 1996), 220.

7. "Auto Workers Offer Film on Tolerance," 16; "Animated Shorts Too Costly, Geo. Pal Also into Feature Prods," *Variety*, November 20, 1946, 19.

8. I. F. Stone, "The Grand Inquisition," *Nation*, November 8, 1947, 493; Bill Melendez to author, January 29, 1998.

9. "Preliminary Outline for Film on *Races of Mankind* Entitled *United We Stand*," Papers of the National Association for the Advancement of Colored People, Library of Congress, Washington, D.C., 4, 11; Alexander Klein to the NAACP, April 8, 1946, ibid., 1.

10. "Preliminary Outline," 3; Lardner et al., "Brotherhood of Man: A Script," 356–57, 359.

11. Klein to NAACP, 1; "Preliminary Outline," 1.

12. Earl Ofari Hutchinson, *Black and Red: Race and Class in Conflict, 1919–1990* (East Lansing: Michigan State University, 1995) 126, 202–3, 225.

13. "Transcription: *Mississippi Hare*," Warner Brothers Archives, University of Southern California, 1.

14. Ibid., 2.

15. Norman M. Klein, *7 Minutes: The Life and Death of the American Animated Cartoon* (London: Verso, 1993), 192, 211; Elaine Tyler May, *Homeward Bound: American Families in the Cold War Era* (New York: Basic Books, 1982), 165.

16. David Riesman, *The Lonely Crowd: A Study of the Changing American Character* (New Haven: Yale University Press), 34.

17. Michael K. Honey, *Southern Labor and Black Civil Rights: Organizing Memphis Workers* (Urbana: University of Illinois Press, 1993), 16.

18. *Daredevil Droopy*, dialogue continuity, February 22, 1949, Metro-Goldwyn-Mayer Collection, University of Southern California Archives, 3.

19. *Mouse Cleaning*, script, March 6, 1947, ibid., 9.

20. May, *Homeward Bound*, 170.

21. *A Mouse in the House*, 3; *Life with Tom*, script, November 19, 1951, Metro-Goldwyn-Mayer Collection, University of Southern California Archives, 4; *Life with Tom*, dialogue sheet, ibid., 7–8.

22. *The Little Orphan*, script, ibid., 4; *Little Wise Quacker*, script, October 25, 1950, ibid., 2; *Little Wise Quacker*, dialogue sheet, ibid.

23. *Droopy's Good Deed*, script, March 25, 1949, ibid., 5; *Droopy's Good Deed*, dialogue sheet, ibid., 1.

24. *Garden Gopher*, script, August 5, 1948, ibid., 2–3.

25. *Magical Maestro*, script, September 29, 1949, ibid., 4.

26. Robert Sklar, *Movie-Made America: A Cultural History of American Movies* (New York: Vintage Books, 1994), 285; Leonard Maltin, *Of Mice and Magic: A History of American Animated Cartoons* (New York: Plume, 1987), 304.

27. Michael Barrier, *Hollywood Cartoons: American Animation in Its Golden Age* (New York: Oxford University Press, 1999), 546.

28. Henry T. Sampson, in *That's Enough, Folks: Black Images in Animated Cartoons, 1900–1960* (Lanham, Md.: Scarecrow Press, 1998), 219–37, provides an alphabetical listed of cartoons that contain images of African Americans. A study of this index reveals that between 1913 and 1954 these images appeared in at least one film per year.

Conclusion

1. Leonard Maltin, *Of Mice and Magic: A History of American Animated Cartoons* (New York: Plume, 1987), 186, 346. Viacom International, which owned the Terrytoons Studio in the 1970s, sold the studio facility on December 29, 1972, according to the records of the Bureau of Assessment of New Rochelle, N.Y.

INDEX

CHRISTOPHER P. LEHMAN is an associate professor in the Ethnic Studies Department at St. Cloud State University, St. Cloud, Minnesota. He was born in Philadelphia and raised in Edmond, Oklahoma. The first African American at Oklahoma State University to finish the Honors Program on graduation, Lehman earned a B.A. with Honors in History. At the University of Massachusetts Amherst he earned an M.A. in History and both an M.A. and a Ph.D. in Afro American Studies. He has published articles in *Journal of Popular Film & Television*, *Historical Journal of Film, Radio, and Television*, and *Journal of Black Studies* and is the author of *American Animated Cartoons of the Vietnam Era: A Study of Social Commentary in Films and Television Programs, 1961–1973*. Christopher Lehman lives in Minnesota with his wife, Rev. Yolanda Lehman, and their daughter Imani.